THE
UNMISTAKABLE
HAND *of* GOD

A partial account of God's hand in my many
experiences as a missionary in Africa and around the world

Roy Comrie

ISBN 978-1-64079-439-9 (Paperback)
ISBN 978-1-64079-440-5 (Digital)

Christian Faith Publishing, Inc.
296 Chestnut Street
Meadville, PA 16335
www.christianfaithpublishing.com

Printed in the United States of America

Oh Lord you are our Father, we are the *clay* and you
are the *potter*, we are formed by your *hand*.

—Isaiah 64:8

CONTENTS

ROY COMRIE—MESSENGER AND MOTIVATOR TO MISSIONARIES

Foreword by Sydney Hudson Reed

Author's note: Sydney Hudson Reed pastored the first church I ever entered in a meaningful way. He wrote a book titled They Came My Way. *He knew of my antagonism and my repentance. He was a patient fisher of men. I am so glad he and Jean came to Rhodesia (Zimbabwe) and cast the Lord's net toward, first, my sister Sheila, then me. The following is what he wrote in his book.*

Roy was part of an outstanding youth group at Salisbury (Harare) Baptist Church in the 1950s. Shy of nature, few would have predicted that he would become a great preacher, but he certainly did. This is how it began.

We had in our congregation an elderly woman who had exercised a voluntary missionary ministry in Israel. She was well equipped for discipling. I have some of her charts in my possession. Her method was to seek out new converts, invite them to her flat for tea, and introduce them to what was a good, sound grounding in the basics of the Christian faith. Roy was not at all sure of what he was being let into, but after a few sessions, he came to appreciate the earnest and profitable teaching that Mrs. Jordan gave.

When I shared the vision of the Church on Wheels with Mrs. Jordan, she responded immediately with a generous donation toward the project, believing that some of her trainees would be launched on their preaching careers in that oversized caravan. Roy was among those who took their first tentative steps into the inestimable privilege of proclaiming the good news in the Church on Wheels. Further training at Rhodes University, the Baptist Theological College, and overseas launched Roy with his greatly supportive wife, Gwyneth, on their missionary career. It eventuated in a ministry of motivation and encouragement to the worldwide family of missionaries serving in the ranks of the AEF and SIM.

My friendship with Roy started through the "right of entry" conceived by Cecil Rhodes, whereby ministers were given the opportunity of scripture teaching in the schools. I had my fair share, having been trained as a teacher. We had an added dimension in our friendship—our mutual love for the game of tennis. It was a great privilege for me to play with an exponent of the game of Roy's caliber. If he had made tennis his first priority, he would have gone far, even beyond playing for his country, Zimbabwe. While at Rhodes University, he won all three events in the tennis championships: singles, doubles, and mixed.

Hearing Roy expounding the scriptures has been a thrill for me and brought the realization that time and energy invested in ministry to the young is never in vain.

THROUGH INSURMOUNTABLE GATES AND WALLS

Foreword by Dr. Jack Taylor

Roy and Gwyn Comrie and their four children—Douglas, Andrew, Janice, and Bruce—have been supported by our church for forty-five years. While I have only walked through these last seventeen years of the journey with this modern-day Daniel, I have witnessed the hand of God in this dynamic and humble servant. Africa's springs have quenched our thirsts in separate countries, but Roy's feet have hardened the pathways of many more villages and people groups.

Turn these pages slowly and swallow these words carefully as you take in what God is still doing today. Roy's story pulls you into the darkest corridors of pain and through the most impossible of barriers to witness what the Almighty does to change the heart of a man or woman.

Why? is a question that drowns our minds with myriad unknowns. *Who!* is a statement that carries us in the shadows of our darkest valleys.

When I sit across the table from Roy and Gwyn, I hear their heart as missionaries, as shepherds, as a brother and sister in Christ. I also hear something else: I hear the awe of those who have walked in the footsteps of Isaiah and John as they witness the glory of a God who will not ignore his own quest to reach the unreachable—to save the unsaveable.

What do you do with a phone call from half a world away informing you of your sister's rape and murder? And how do you gain the strength to fly, grieve, and lead that funeral service? How do you dare meet, share, forgive, and learn to love her murderer as a brother in Christ? You will meet the answers in these pages.

Roy's convictions and confidence in Jesus didn't come from growing up in a comfortable Christian environment. The tangible life changes in his younger sister, Sheila, and her friends wooed him toward Jesus. His familiarity with the hard side of life tempered him with a deep grace and gentleness toward others who still stumble in their journey. Being welcomed into someone else's painful journey is a mercy that draws us through our own confusions with the sovereign plan of our Maker.

Roy's early physical training in tennis, Highland dance, and soccer (football) prepared him for a rigorous and demanding schedule as he began to travel through his beloved Africa preaching the Word. That inner drive to persevere and endure despite the challenges continues to carry him through many times when others would quit.

Under a campaign led by Anglican minister John Stott in Rhodes University, Roy confirmed his call to full-time ministry and has never looked back. Gwyn was one of the fourteen students who set themselves apart at that time. Their courtship began in earnest when they were called to be counselors at the same camp, and through this experience, Roy affirms repeatedly that we should always be willing to trace the hand of God in any leading or calling.

God's path to glory often takes strange twists. What can you say when you encounter a Bible that survives a fire that reduces everything around it to ashes, a paralyzing black mamba bite that takes Roy to the brink of death, the curses of the Vananga Valubuko (powerful witch doctor) who calls lightning from the sky, the beating and rape of a missionary woman by a vicious thief, amebic dysentery in a child hundreds of miles from medical care, flooded roads that swallow your vehicle, wars and martyrs, the death of children in a vehicle accident—moments attributable only to the hand of God. It is the stuff of desperate prayer.

While Roy's impact extends into Zambia, Congo, Angola, Zimbabwe, Malawi, and other African nations through those he has trained and ministered to, it is his commitment to prayer and to the loving unity of the Spirit among believers that forms a foundation for the power of God in his life and experience. The impact isn't constrained to Africa. Roy explains in his book how a revival in North Korea began through a role he played in Africa.

Roy is always on duty. Whether in hospital with his own life-and-death drama, deep in a jungle faced with dark spiritual forces, weaving back and forth on dirt roads mined to destroy, or preaching to church folk and missionaries, he humbly searches for the opportunities that God brings his way. Without manipulation, he speaks straightforward truth and finds joy in each proclamation.

Name after name appears on these pages to remind us that every person is important to Roy and to the Lord he serves. Worthy acts are remembered and shared for all of us to celebrate the goodness of God for those who acted without expectation of recognition. Some of these names are written in heaven as martyrs. The name that appears everywhere, behind almost every other name on these pages, is that of Jesus.

Some have questioned the wisdom of raising four children in the face of venomous snakes, rocket attacks, and life-threatening diseases. Roy and Gwyn committed early that being in the center of God's will was the safest place to be. They still live this way.

As pastor at large, Roy has traveled frequently through war zones and isolated centers to care for the servants of Christ in the fourteen African countries under his care. His speaking at spiritual life conferences in Africa, South America, and Asia has encouraged many to remain steady on their knees and faithful in their service.

By living themselves in the middle of the impossible, the Comries are still able to minister to other servants of God who are freshly immersed in the shadows of situations beyond human understanding. The verses of Acts 29 are still being written. This book is evidence for all to see the hidden hand of the real author behind the story.

As Roy states, "When we agree to see and participate in what God is doing, we can only stand back in amazement. The unmistakable hand of God can be seen in every step of this journey."

ACKNOWLEDGMENTS

Ordinary people, clay which is local or from a foreign country. It is still ordinary, it is still just clay, but in the master's hand, Simon becomes Peter, Abram becomes Abraham. The master transforms the ordinary, and events in our lives unfold in a series of purposes that point to the unmistakable presence of the one who said, "it is not by might or power but by my spirit." Thank you Lord for the privilege of looking in on how you transform the ordinary in answer to prayer.

Thank you my sweetheart, my closest friend, my wife for life. You breathed every paragraph, lived every line. You could have and probably should have written this book. Your encouragement and partnership especially in the school of prayer, is amazing. The intimacies of marriage, precious as they are, are exceeded by the intimacies of togetherness around his throne. Every person in these pages was carefully prayed over and together we give our loving, Heavenly Father all the glory.

To our twenty nine personal prayer and financial supporters in Canada, Africa, Britain and Australia and to our seven churches in Ontario, three in British Columbia and others in South Africa and Zimbabwe. To most in this grouping of individuals and churches your partnership lasted over fifty years. Thank you Lord, you taught us so much from their perseverance.

To Will Walker our friend and fellow missionary. Your journalistic editing skills and spiritual insights brought light into some dark corners. Thanks to you too, Madelaine for your kind hospitality.

To our SIM and old AEF families in Canada and around the world and especially to Dorothy and Helen in their respective International offices. You brought not only direction but loving care.

To John and Brian in Faith Christian Publishing and to the editors and staff. Thank you for your patience and wise encouragement..

Finally to Mike Brandon, my Zimbabwe teenage friend. You bridged the gap between AEF and SIM and served on both boards for forty seven years. Your spiritual and financial care and counsel could never be measured. As you battle terminal pancreatic cancer we sit at your feet and learn not only how to live right but how to die like the soldier of Jesus Christ that you are. We love you Ruth and Mike and are amazed at his grace given during your present trials.

INTRODUCTION

It seems hypocritical to write under the title above when, up to the age of seventeen, I had nothing but a prejudiced view of the mind, heart, will, and purpose of God. I grew up in an unbelieving family with very loose connections to the Presbyterian Church and was certainly not interested in God or spiritual things at all. I had my future all planned out, and nothing was going to deter me from pursuing it. But God, in mercy, had other ideas. I now have the firm conviction, as I write, that every moment of my childhood and teenage years came not only under the scrutiny but also under the loving care and kindness of our just and loving Heavenly Father.

What follows is the unfolding story of how God has led us over the past fifty years. I am amazed as I recount our many experiences as missionaries in Africa, how the hand of God can be seen everywhere. I am humbled and grateful how God has used Gwyn and me to serve Him and to touch so many lives with His love. When I talk about "unmistakable," it references God, not us. We stand amazed at His mercy, forgiveness, and patience. We are utterly unworthy of any of His interventions in our lives. We completely acknowledge our own humanity, our own weakness and failure. The spiritual battles right up to this moment have never ceased. "It is not by might or by power, but by My Spirit, says the Lord Almighty" (Zech.4:6). What a privilege it has been to travel so extensively and to share God's love and to witness His interventions with so many.

The stories I tell are not necessarily in chronological order. Neither are they about me, but about our great, wonderful, and caring God. It is His hand that has been on us, and it has been His involvement in every detail of our lives that we can confidently say, "It is not I but Christ who lives in me."

The story really begins when God began His work in my family and in me by bringing the youngest member of our family, Sheila, at the age of fifteen, into a vital relationship with Himself. She brought His light into a very dark, antagonistic place. Whatever she had done changed her life.

My parents were not interested and very dismissive of what Sheila was experiencing. They saw it as a fad, an emotional journey. Though I had a very close bond with Sheila, I could see this as dividing us. I was categorical in my rejection of God, but Sheila brought her joyful girlfriends to our home, and you couldn't doubt the reality of what they were experiencing in the Lord. It was puzzling to see so many beautiful girls all being taken in by this illusion. Surely, I thought, Sheila would soon return to the real world.

The stories that follow have been used in conferences, churches, Bible colleges, universities, home groups, and schools around the world. I always seek to exposit the Word of God and follow the example of Jesus, the master storyteller, in bringing up-to-date examples of His unmistakable hand moving in the everyday events of our lives or of those with whom we were serving. Many have asked for these to be written, and as portions have been published in magazines, folks have phoned or e-mailed to say that they effectively used the stories in their prison or other ministries. More effective than that, these stories have been used in personal evangelism and counseling.

So I will begin my story with Sheila's story, at the puzzling juncture of her murder. Be patient. The gaps will be filled in, and the focus restored.

Chapter 1

SHEILA

Unless a grain of wheat falls into the earth and dies,
it remains alone; but if it dies, it bears much fruit.

—John 12:24

After an extended tour of ministry in four different countries, Gwyn and I were exhausted and thankful to get back to our home in Abbotsford, British Columbia. It was July 2007, and we were looking forward to connecting with family and friends.

But life was about to change dramatically. Less than a week later, early in the morning, we received a call from my nephew Craig in Zimbabwe, the eldest son of my younger sister, Sheila. He had just been notified that his mother had been brutally raped and murdered in her little home in Hibberdene on the KwaZulu south coast of South Africa.

It was so hard for us to believe it as just two months earlier, we had spent five wonderful days with Sheila in that same little home. Craig, who lived in a suburb of Harare, Zimbabwe, was in total shock, as were we. He had already decided that he and his wife and family would leave for South Africa as soon as they could. His younger brother Neil—who lived in Grafton, Queensland, Australia—with his wife, Penny, and two daughters, was already making plans to fly to South Africa as soon as their bookings could be arranged.

"Uncle Roy," said Craig before we hung up, "would you come to South Africa and take the funeral?" Little did I know of the adventure God would be taking me on when I agreed to Craig's request.

When our son Douglas, a pilot with a regional airline under Air Canada, heard the news, the airline gave him time off to organize standby tickets for me to fly to South Africa. I was able to fly out that night on the only seat available on a 747 flight from Vancouver to London, England. From London, I again got the last seat on a flight to Nairobi. A mercy seat was miraculously found for me on the flight from Nairobi to Johannesburg. By the time I arrived in Johannesburg, I was exhausted. Just as I was heading out of the airport to find a bed and much-needed sleep, suddenly, out of nowhere, a young man approached me.

"The plane for Durban is taking off in fifteen minutes," he spoke urgently. He pointed to the check in desk. "They will give you the gate number and are holding the plane for you. Hurry."

There was no time to think as I hurried off. My mind was racing and full of questions. As I ran for the departure gate, I wondered, *Lord, was that an angel? How did he know that I was going to Durban?* Why would they hold the plane for someone with a standby ticket and who had not yet checked in? It had to be an angel!

I was welcomed on board as the last passenger.

There was more to come! When I walked into the car hire in Durban, I was greeted enthusiastically by the lady in charge. She had been transferred from Johannesburg to Durban and remembered me from previous trips. When she heard about my circumstances, she gave me an unbelievable deal on a small compact car and then promptly gave me an upgrade at no extra cost.

I drove down that beautiful coast, grieving deeply for the loss of my sister Sheila. At the age of fifteen, she had become the first one in our family to experience new life in Christ. I remember her being overwhelmingly in love with the Lord and deeply concerned for those around her, including me.

"Roy," she said, "you have got to come and hear this message. This is not about religion. It's about a relationship with the living God!"

I remember mocking her and thinking, *This isn't for me*. Besides, I had my life all planned out. God was certainly not a part of it, or so I thought. But eventually, as I saw the transformation in her life, I relented and went to hear what she was so excited about. At first, I still resisted what I was hearing, but it's hard to resist the compelling love of our Heavenly Father. So it wasn't long before I finally repented and found the wonder of having a deep, personal relationship with the Lord and the best gift of all, forgiveness. In time, my mother believed, and then my dad made a commitment. From being an alcoholic, he never touched another drink. My parents had ten wonderful years of marriage before my father died. Later, my older sister, Heather, found the Lord on her deathbed. We had so much for which to thank Sheila.

Sadly, after Sheila had walked so closely with the Lord for nearly five years, a man in the church approached her sexually. Afraid and confused, she ran. How could this happen within the church, the very place we should feel safe and protected? But hypocrisy can be found everywhere. The church is not immune from it.

Sheila later married her beloved John, but neither of them wanted anything to do with hypocritical "religion." Tragically, after many years of marriage, John succumbed to cancer. A few months after John died, Sheila once again began to pursue a relationship with the Lord. In May 2007, we spent five days with her and were thrilled to know that she was reading her Bible and other helpful books and finding strength and hope in prayer. Now she had been brutally murdered, and yet I found solace in the knowledge that she was with her Lord, seeing Him face-to-face.

My thoughts once again focused on the journey I was making. I calculated that I had been traveling in one way or another for over thirty hours. Grief and fatigue kept overtaking me, and the road ahead became blurred. I needed to stop and sleep before I could face Craig and Jenny and their children—Lindsay, Sarah, and Andrew—as well as Neil, Sheila's second son. All of them would want help with grieving as well as answers to many questions.

I stopped in the next town, Scotborough, and drove toward the sea and the first hotel I could find. Before I went to sleep, I told the Lord what He already knew: that I was utterly weak and rather fearful, and that I desperately needed His promise to be fulfilled from Isaiah 40:31, that I would be able to mount up with wings like an eagle, to run and not be weary, to walk and not faint. After a brief meal, I was able to sleep for a few hours before completing the journey to where Sheila had lived for many years.

The next two days were extraspecial with Sheila's family. We spent time processing the horrifying details of her death as outlined by her friends who found her. We wept together. Our times of reminiscing and remembering were painful yet comforting in their own way. I cannot recall giving any profound answers to the *why* questions, but we did speak about the Bible found next to her bed, along with Christian novels and devotional books, which gave further testimony to Sheila's renewed delight in her Lord. I shared all we had experienced just two months before when Gwyn and I had stayed with Sheila for five days. I am so glad that on the cross, Jesus cried out to His Father, "My God, my God, why have you forsaken me?" The truth is, He never forsakes us. It just feels that way. But trying to find the answer to that *why* gives us an understanding of every other *why* that seems to come up with regularity during our days on this earth.

Sheila's funeral was on a Friday. It was the toughest funeral I have ever taken. Through the tears, I battled for the words and the freedom to speak them and to stay in control of my emotions. I traced Sheila's journey. Spiritually, it was similar to most of the people present, that of human frailty and the failure of the organization of religion. I spoke from John 14:1–6 and the amazing invitation of the crucified, risen Lord to enter a true relationship with Him who has authority over life and death.

So many people came up to me after the service and said that they dared not go to sleep that night without first making their peace with God. There were two people at the funeral who had known Sheila since the day she had turned to Christ and had prayed for her and maintained contact down the years, believing that she would come back into fellowship with her Lord. What precious friends.

The Power of Forgiveness

The next challenge that I faced was the matter of forgiveness. Long after I had flown back home, I wrestled with this and knew that I had to make some decisions. It was Sir George Bernard Shaw who said that forgiveness was a beggar's refuge and that he would have none of it. The truth is, I am a beggar who desperately needs to be forgiven, and I am grateful that the Lord bore the burden so that I could be forgiven and therefore learn to forgive. Naturally, we prayed that the man who had perpetrated this horrific crime would be caught and brought to trial, but would I be able to face him and forgive him?

Down through the years in our ministry experience in Zambia and Zimbabwe, God gave us many illustrations of the deeper meaning of forgiveness. The one that stands out and became pertinent in the follow-up to Sheila's story related to nine of our friends and their four children, who lived just twelve kilometers from us when we were living in Umtali (Mutare) on the eastern border of Zimbabwe. They were missionaries with the Elim Mission and lived up in the Vumba Mountains where they taught at a secondary school.

June 23, 1978, will be forever etched in my memory. It was during the war years in Zimbabwe and in the middle of the night that a group of "freedom fighters" entered the school grounds and herded the missionaries and their children down to a soccer field. They were told they were going to be killed. I can just imagine the emotions they were feeling at that moment. The missionaries asked if they could have time to pray. The following is some of the content of that prayer: "Lord, we are not here because we want to be but because you have allowed us to be here. We pray for these young men. Would you have mercy on them and would you save them. Give us the strength to die for you." Not wanting any gunfire to be heard, the group were hacked to death with axes, even down to a three-week-old baby, Pamela Grace. She was the daughter of Roy and Joyce Lynn, who had married in their thirties and marveled at the gift of a beautiful baby girl. One needs the big picture of eternity to be able to process the ugliness of man's inhumanity to man.

The murders shocked the world, but especially the Christian world. These weren't the first Christians to be murdered in Zimbabwe, but they were our friends. It became very personal and close to home.

As the mission authorities and the relatives began to arrive from England for the funeral, so too did the news media from around the world. At the funeral, there were nine big coffins and four small ones. Heartbreak and triumph were tangled together. So many questions. Why did God allow this? And how do you forgive those who commit such brutal murders, especially on children? I will never forget what the mother of Wendy White, one of the missionaries murdered, said, "I feel I am the most privileged mother in the world to have been called to give my daughter as a martyr for Jesus Christ." What incredible grace!

As we prayed, talked, and grieved, we had, in the end, simply said, "Father, we do not understand, but we choose to trust you. Would you please forgive the young men who did this. They did not know what they were doing. Father, would you follow them and find them and save them. We know that you have a purpose in this tragedy and that the blood of the martyrs has always been the seed of the church."

Little did we know how wonderfully God would answer these prayers.

From Tragedy to Triumph

In the follow-up to that attack, two of the gang were killed and two captured. Thirteen survived to the end of the war.

The commander of the group that killed these missionaries and their children is a man by the name of Garry Hove. At the end of the war, he met a missionary who began to witness to him. "Do not speak to me about forgiveness. My hands are full of blood," said Garry. The missionary took this violent young man to passages in the Bible that showed the violence that Jesus endured in the process of purchasing our salvation so that he could be forgiven, such as Isaiah 52:14: "There were many who were appalled at Him, His appearance was so disfigured beyond that of any man." Although Christ's mental and spiritual sufferings were more intense than the physical, it was the physical that got Garry's attention.

In answer to the prayers of the people he had murdered and their loved ones who had extended forgiveness, Garry came to that cross, and as he repented, the burden of that guilt was lifted, and he experienced the joy of forgiveness and the wonder of being accepted as a child of God. He was given a commission from God through His Word. It was to search out those he had led in violence and murder and tell them about God's love and forgiveness. In the space of two and a half years, he found eight of them and led them to faith in Christ. Seven of the nine, including Garry, went into full-time Christian service.

We had the pleasure of meeting Garry at a service in a Harare church in 1988. As he preached and shared his testimony, we marveled at the faithfulness and forgiveness of God and the adequacy of the redemption found in Christ. Ten years had passed since the murder of our friends, and now Garry's life and story began to touch the lives of multitudes around the world, including the young Zulu man who murdered my sister Sheila.

Meeting Sheila's Murderer

An experienced team of detectives tracked down Chris Mnguni. His prints and DNA were on record as he had previously been imprisoned for break and entry. He had escaped from that prison, and it was while he was on the run that he had committed the atrocities of rape and murder against Sheila. When we heard of his capture, we began to pray more earnestly for him. As the months went by, our burden for him grew.

When a ministry trip to Zimbabwe and South Africa loomed large, we wondered whether a visit to the prison would be a possibility. Before we left on the trip, different ministry requests came in, and our calendar began to fill up. But two requests stood out. On Sunday, February 22, 2009, I was scheduled to preach in a church in

Port Shepstone, not far from where Sheila had lived. From February 25 to the March 1, we were scheduled to be at a missions conference in Scottsville in Pietermaritzburg. This was not far from the maximum-security prison in Westville in which Sheila's alleged murderer was being held. On our calendar, we had set aside February 23 as the day that we would attempt, by the grace of God, to see Chris Mnguni. Those working on our behalf reported that it would be impossible to get into the murder-plus block of Westville Prison as even chaplains were not allowed in.

On Friday, February 20, Geoff Hartley, the pastor of the church in Port Shepstone, called to say that he had been notified that the accused was coming up for his first trial in the High Court in Ramsgate at 9:00 a.m. on the twenty-third! This was truly amazing. He was going to be brought over one hundred kilometers to just within ten minutes of where we were staying, and where I would be preaching. As we approached the place where Sheila had been living, we stopped in for tea with two couples who had been close friends of hers. They had not heard about the trial but promised to pray. The next day, as I preached in the Port Shepstone church, the whole congregation heard the story and promised to pray for Geoff, their pastor, and for me as we went to the trial hearing.

Twenty minutes before the trial was to begin, we met with the detective chief inspector who had led the team in running down the accused. He carried a huge file of evidence.

"Sir," I said, "I am the brother of the murdered woman. Would it be possible for me to have a word with the accused?"

He looked at me with pity and horror and said that it would be impossible. He repeated that word a number of times so that I asked whether there was someone else who would consider my plea. He was obviously irritated, and I could not blame him, but he did lead me inside the court and seated me in the back row while he went to speak to the prosecutor. She was standing in the front and talking on her cell phone. It just so happened that she was speaking to the black judge who was phoning to say that he would be twenty-five minutes late. He had put her in charge and said that if anything came up, she was to deal with it.

The detective presented my plea. She said that my request would be against normal procedure, but given that there was time, she gave three provisos: one, the defense lawyer had to agree; two, the prisoner had to agree; and three, that everything that I, as the brother of the murdered woman said, would have to be recorded and witnessed.

The two of them went over to the defense lawyer with the story. He looked back at me and agreed. They then went over to the prisoner. He heard, looked back at me, and amazingly, he agreed.

The meeting could not take place in the high court, so a small back room was chosen. There was only one bench along a wall, and I was seated right next to the prisoner, along with his guard and a translator. The prosecutor, the defense lawyer, two detectives, the court clerk, and a couple of others stood around us to witness this proceeding. They started the recorder and signaled to me to begin.

I introduced myself to Chris Mnguni as the brother of the woman he was alleged to have murdered. If I had not said *alleged*, they would have stopped the proceedings immediately. I then told him that I wanted to tell him a story of how a murderer of my friends later became my brother. I then began to relate the story of Garry Hove and the murder of those nine missionaries and their four children. Halfway through this story, I looked up. The detective chief inspector had tears running down his cheeks. He spoke to me later and said he had been a detective for a long time but had never heard or seen anything like this. I realized that the Lord had bigger plans than I could have imagined. I felt just a tiny bit like that missionary Paul who shared the good news of forgiveness to another professional legal grouping.

When I had completed the story, I gave the prisoner a Bible in his own Zulu language and told him where to start reading it. He looked me in the eye and said, "I am so sorry."

The cry went up that the judge had arrived. We all hurried through to the main court and stood as the judge entered. The plea of "not guilty" sounded so hollow, and I realized that there was still a long way to go. The prisoner was remanded in custody pending the appointment of a new defense lawyer. The next case was called.

The prisoner and his guard shuffled toward the back entrance where a prison security vehicle was supposed to be waiting. Geoff and I headed for his car in the parking lot. I looked back and saw the prisoner and his guard waiting on the sidewalk (pavement). The security vehicle still had not arrived. I did not say anything to Geoff but walked toward the prisoner and his guard. To approach the man accused of murdering your sister outside the court would have been unthinkable in most countries, but when I approached the guard and asked if I could have another word with the prisoner, he was agreeable as he had heard my story inside and knew that I was not seeking vengeance but forgiveness. "The prison security vehicle is supposed to be here," he said. "You can speak while we wait."

I had prepared for the first encounter with the prisoner, but now I had no idea what I would say. With a quick prayer to the Lord, I started to speak. "Your name is Chris Mnguni," I said. "But I am sure that you have another deep Zulu name."

"Yes," he said, "my Zulu name is Sthenjwa."

At that moment, I knew what the Lord wanted me to say. "Today," I said, "you stood before a man who is going to be your judge. The prosecutor is going to try and get a conviction, and the defense lawyer is going to try and get you acquitted. I do not know which way it will go, but there is another judge. He is the judge of all the earth. He will judge you, your guard, and me. When you stand before Him, you will need a defense lawyer, and His name is Jesus Christ. He has already paid the price to set you free and to forgive every wrong thing that you have done. The price was His own life-blood, which was shed for all mankind. God the Father was satisfied with His sacrifice, and on the third day, Jesus was raised from the dead. He now lives in the hearts of millions of people around the world who call Him their Savior."

The security vehicle drowned out any more conversation, and Chris was whisked away.

I walked slowly back to where Geoff was waiting. My heart was filled with thankfulness to the Lord. "Lord," I said, "they said it was impossible, but I thank you that you are the God of the impossible. You made the judge late and gave me acceptance with the prosecutor, the defense lawyer, and the prisoner. You made the security vehicle late and gave me the words to say to Chris."

As we drove back, Geoff said, "Roy, that was God. We could never have gotten anywhere without Him today."

Both of us were overcome with emotion and praise.

The Adventure Continues

All that happened in February 2009. In August 2009, I was back in Zimbabwe for some very special meetings and then flew to South Africa.

I had never met Andy Munro until the August 30, 2009. We had been corresponding by e-mail for some months, and as a prison chaplain, he had sought to make contact with Chris Mnguni but had not been allowed entrance to that maximum-security murder-plus section of Westville Prison. I told him I was coming from Canada via Zimbabwe and would arrive at his house in Pietermaritzburg on the thirtieth. Could he arrange with Westville Prison for me to see the man who allegedly murdered my sister Sheila, and would he have time to accompany me?

He had phoned the prison and spoken to the director, telling him that the brother of the woman who was murdered allegedly by one of his prisoners was coming, and could he visit Chris Mnguni?

"Chaplain Munro," the director said, "you know the rules. It is not possible. Do not phone me again. If something can be worked out, I will phone you."

When I arrived in Pietermaritzburg, Andy apologized for his failure in getting things lined up. The director had not phoned back. Do we just go and get in line? I had come a long way and was committed to trying. Andy, thankfully, agreed to accompany me.

If I had not been told it was a prison, I would have thought it was a university, except for the high walls and electric fences. It was a massive structure and spread over many acres. When we saw the lineup of relatives waiting to see inmates, Andy estimated that it was a six-hour wait. I said I would stay but would understand if he wanted to leave. Encouragingly, Andy stayed.

We had only been in the line for about five minutes when a uniformed man came out of the main building and marched down the line toward us. "Is there a Mr. Comrie here?" he shouted."

In shock, I put my hand up. No explanation was given, but we were taken to the front of the queue to confirm our identity. We were searched thoroughly, making the average airport search seem like child's play! We then went through three of the most amazing sets of iron gates, each one closing ominously behind us. We went down a passage to a large room with some plain benches and one man at a desk. We were asked to wait on the back bench while they went to call the prisoner. There was some alarm when he could not be found, but the man at the desk suggested that he was probably on a work detail. They eventually found him in a small Christian meeting in the company of three other men.

As Chris was brought into the room and came toward us, Andy, who speaks Zulu fluently, began to talk to him. Pointing to me, he asked, "Do you know this man?"

"Yes," he said, "that is the brother. He came to my first trial. He told me a story of a man in Zimbabwe, and he also gave me a Bible in my language. I have been reading it every day."

I asked him a number of questions to find out where he was spiritually. Eventually, Andy said to me, "Roy, we do not need any more questions. This guy if for real."

We marveled at the grace of God. Before we ever got there, God had brought Chris to Himself. The man who had murdered someone so special to me was now my brother in the Lord. The Garry Hove story was being repeated again. How great is our God!

We sought to encourage Chris, giving him a number of books in Zulu that would explain how to grow in the Christian faith. I also gave him a songbook in Zulu. Among African tribes, they produce some of the greatest harmony. We prayed with Chris before he went out.

A Door Opens

Waiting at the door were three other prisoners who were convicted murderers. They had come to faith through Christian radio programs. When they found Chris reading his Bible, they had helped him understand the way of salvation. I spoke to Ricky, an Indian man; and Andy spoke to the other two, who were Zulus. Their faith shone out, and we told them that we would pray for them as they sought to represent Christ in this desperate place.

No sooner had they left us when in walked the director, the deputy director, and the head of Social Services. We were speechless! After greeting one another, the director spoke to me. "Mr. Comrie, we just want to thank you for your attitude."

"My attitude?" I asked, somewhat confused. "What do you mean?"

"Your attitude of forgiveness," explained the director. "Because of your attitude, this prisoner has been able to find forgiveness and peace with God."

Andy and I realized at exactly the same time that the African director of Westville Prison was a Christian, and we marveled at the privilege God was giving to us.

The head of Social Services was an African lady, and Andy, with his background in sociology, was delighted to share with her how he incorporated that subject into his teaching of prisoners. Andy had brought the course with him, so he showed it to the lady and then to the director.

"Sir," Andy said to the director, "Mr. Comrie is going back to Canada, but I stay here in South Africa. We met with four of the men in this cellblock today. Would it be possible for me to return here and teach them this course?"

Immediately, he responded, "Chaplain Munro, just phone me, and I will make the arrangements for you."

What had been impossible just moments before was now an open door.

We were again shown through those three iron gates, and once outside, we looked at each other with tears in our eyes as the goodness of our God overwhelmed us.

"You know, Roy," said Andy, "only God could have gotten us in and out of this facility today."

When Gates and Walls Seem Insurmountable

It was to be another year before I would be in South Africa again. Our next ministry trip was planned for October 2010. As our speaking schedule began to fill, my granddaughter Michelle asked me to conduct her wedding on November 20, 2010. I was delighted. Theirs is a true love story, and I felt honored to marry them. As I write, this Paul and Michelle are the proud parents of our first two great-grandchildren.

The events of Friday, January 7, 2011 were to become another milestone in our journey of forgiveness and our growing relationship with Chris Mnguni. So much prayer by so many people had gone into this day. This was going to be my fourth meeting with Chris. Each time, a pastor or a prison chaplain had accompanied me, but Andy Munro was on a much-needed vacation, and so I was going in alone. I knew that my Heavenly Father would be going with me, but somehow I thought that because I had done this before, I certainly would not need a miracle. I was wrong.

My car was one of only three in the huge parking lot, and no long lines were visible. My delight in being able to go straight up to the man at the gate was short-lived when he told me that this Friday was a lockdown day. No visitors were allowed, and there were no exceptions! I was told to come back tomorrow. My heart sank. My program was full, and I had no tomorrows to give. Those gates and walls suddenly seemed insurmountable. Would I have to wait another year before seeing Chris?

Then it struck me. I know the director. At least I could check in with him and just maybe, because I had come all the way from Canada, he would bend the rules just a fraction and allow me a fleeting visit. I boldly broached the question. The director, I was told, was an extremely busy man, especially on lockdown day.

However, the curiosity of the man at the front gate got the better of him, and he asked what it was that made me so keen to visit a prisoner that day. There was no one in a line behind me, so I told him the story of my sister Sheila and her murderer, and the subsequent events that led him into a living relationship with the Lord and a growing relationship with me. He doubted that it would help, but he gave me a pass to murder plus.

The gatekeeper at murder plus was irritated that a pass had been issued and reiterated the "no visitation, no exception" rule. The request to see the director was met with an incredulous, cold stare. He was kept busy with locking and unlocking the Iron Gate for prison staff coming and going. He warned me that I might have to wait the whole day until the director was about to go home. I indicated my willingness to wait.

"What is so important on the inside of this prison that would keep you waiting all day?" he asked.

I recounted the story once again, and he instantly became my ally, wanting to facilitate my entry. He thought he heard the director's voice and rushed in to see whether he could make an appointment for me, but it was not the director. He then said he would let me into the director's office to wait for him there. "It will be much more comfortable," he said. I thankfully accepted his offer.

I was not seated for more than a minute when in walked a man with many pips on his shoulders. He introduced himself as the area director, Dladla Msizi Patrick. I do not understand the South African prison system, but I concluded that he was even more important than the director! He said that the director was not available but that he would hear my request. I was grief-stricken as I realized that he knew none of the background and was obviously a very busy man.

I gave him the short hurried version of my story. His reply was brief, respectful, but decisive. "I have heard you. We will have to check out the truthfulness of what you have said. When is your next visit from Canada to South Africa?" I replied that we hoped it would be sometime in 2012. "If your story checks out," he said, "we will ensure that you see the prisoner when you come next year."

I knew that I was being dismissed, and my heart was heavy. But the unmistakable hand of God was at work. At that moment, in walked the deputy director, the man whom Andy and I had met on our last visit. He greeted me warmly and even remembered my name. "Sir," he said to the area director, "the director, the social worker, and I met with Chaplain Munro and Mr. Comrie last year. Have you heard his story?"

What had seemed impossible moments before was becoming possible.

"I obviously have not heard enough of the story," said the area director. "So perhaps you better start from the beginning."

With renewed hope, I began to relate the story, starting with Sheila's untimely death and telling in detail the amazing intervention of our Heavenly Father at Chris Mnguni's first trial, which enabled me to speak to him for seventeen minutes after being told that speaking to him would be impossible. I then followed up with the subsequent visit with Andy Munro and how amazingly the way was opened for us to visit with Chris in murder plus. The area director was particularly interested in this visit.

Suddenly the area director sat forward in his chair with his hands on his knees. Not looking at me, he began to shake his head from side to side. "There is no way that you are not going to get into this prison today," he said. The double negative threw me for a moment, and then I realized, as I looked at his smile, that it was a wonderfully positive statement.

A message was sent to bring the prisoner down to his office. I wondered if my visit with Chris Mnguni was going to be witnessed by the area director and the deputy director? Not that I minded, but it seemed strange. While we were waiting for Chris to be brought down, the area director told me about his family, and then he explained the psychology behind their prison policy. Having observed the relaxed freedoms on the inside of the prison, I was deeply interested. I am still uncertain as to whether this approach is applied to all prisons in all South Africa or only in the KwaZulu area. As I understand it, the policy is one of building honor and trust. Even within the confines of murder plus, prisoners were allowed privileges and freedoms. One example given was that in one area, there could be as many as five hundred prisoners with only four unarmed guards. Abuse of privilege would lead to severe penalties. I understand that this nonlegalistic system is working beyond expectation.

In keeping with their policy, Chris arrived uncuffed and accompanied by his guard. The guard remembered me from the last visit and was warm in his greeting. The area director asked the guard about the behavior and character of the prisoner.

"Sir," he said, "he is a model prisoner who has grown in every area of cooperation."

The area director then addressed the prisoner in Zulu, and I suspected that he was questioning him about the details of the story and the reality of his so-called conversion. He seemed satisfied with the replies.

"Mr. Comrie," he said, "this is a story that needs to be documented." He asked if I would agree if things could be arranged to produce a documentary on this story. I left him with my contact details. The area director shook me warmly by the hand, and I followed Chris and his guard into a room deep in the prison.

Chris and I were alone for just over an hour. On a lockdown day, God gave me what I did not deserve in meaningful witness to people in authority and to Chris. He eagerly received the books in Zulu that I had brought to encourage him in his walk with the Lord. He is so desirous in being a good witness in that prison. Whenever Sheila's name was mentioned, both hands came over his head, and as he bowed in shame, he would say, "If only I had known what I now know, I would never have taken those drugs and committed that terrible crime."

As I came out of the prison again and into the sunshine of South Africa, I marveled once more at our Heavenly Father's favor in allowing me to participate with Him in the details of that day. The *why* questions that I have never been fully able to answer to Sheila's sons, their wives, and their children may one day be answered when we will know Him even as we are known, and see the fruit that came out of the tragic death when He shows us the other side of that divine embroidery.

Chapter 2

MY GROWING YEARS

Granny Robertson

Grandpa Robertson appeared half a dozen times in my boyhood. He and Granny were separated but never divorced. He was a master builder, loved by the ladies, tall, muscular, and often photographed in a manly pose. Granny never complained about him but would never live with him. Their son, my uncle Bill, got his height and good looks from him, but was the easiest-going, nicest guy. I envied my cousins Lynn, John, and Sandy because their dad came home every night. Fun and laughter accompanied every meal, and they were rich with my aunt Isobel coming from the MacDonald clan, who owned half of Bulawayo, or so it seemed to me!

Granny Robertson, my mom's mom, lived with us from as far back as I could remember. I loved her as dearly as I loved my mum, and even more when my parents disciplined me. Somehow her presence made all the difference. She taught me three things: to knit, Scottish country dancing, and Robbie Burns's poems.

Granny and I would sit together on our front verandah, and all you could hear was the click of needles. She would sew the squares together, and these blankets and balaclavas were sent to needy soldiers who were fighting off Hitler. I once won ten shillings from the

Walter Robin children's club for the neatest and most squares. With my prize money, I remember buying seven books and treating myself and a friend to a cowboy movie featuring Roy Rogers. Granny's good works were known all over Salisbury (Harare), and everybody seemed to know her. She was always laughing; maybe that is where my uncle Bill got it.

My two sisters, Heather and Sheila, and I were the best dancers in the Caledonian society of Rhodesia. Heather was chosen to dance the Highland fling for the royal visit to Rhodesia in 1947. I remember being upset because Granny had told me that I was a better dancer than Heather. She later added that Heather was a lot bonnier! It eventually clicked that a lot of my athletic ability came from learning to leap in Scottish country dancing. I was not only good at dancing the Highland fling but also the Gay Gordons, the eightsome reel, strip the willow, and the Dashing White Sergeant. In my mind, I still go through some of those wonderful steps. Years later, when my wife and I were on our honeymoon in Scotland, while watching the finals of the country dancing, I could remember every step and the height of every leap.

Granny regularly and dramatically quoted Robbie Burns's poems. Many lines still meander through my mind, and I boasted that there was no part of the Scots brogue that was beyond my ability to understand. That, however, is no longer true. I am not hearing enough good Scots being spoken!

Granny was never sick until she was seventy-three, and the family doctor came only to announce that she be admitted to hospital. She dug in her heels and announced that she had had her three score years and ten with a bonus of three and that she did not need the help being offered and was prepared to meet her Maker. The next day, she requested to see each one of us in turn. My grief was too great to recall what she said to me, but I do remember her raised voice telling my dad that he was a fool to allow alcohol to ruin his life and bring such heartache to our family. She died that night, and I have often wondered how she did that as she appeared to still have so much strength and energy.

The void she left was immense. Mum was devastated, and I discovered that I had lost one of my keenest supporters as I played in junior tennis tournaments all over Southern Africa. My knitting partner was also gone!

My Dad

My dad, James Harris Comrie, was born in Comrie in Perth shire, Scotland. It is a small town often voted as the most beautiful in the British Isles. His early years were in Aberdeen, and then the family left the hardships of Scotland for the sunny skies and boundless opportunities of South Africa. As a master builder, his dad, Peter (married to Flora), was quickly rewarded with a stable income from a country screaming for development. Interestingly enough, my grandpa Peter's four brothers headed for Canada and one to Oregon in the USA. There may be more Comries now in North America than in Scotland.

After Dad had completed his high school, he went to night school for engineering studies. He sailed alone to Scotland to complete his engineering qualifications and, after graduation, landed a good job with the Vacuum Oil Company of South Africa.

I later read many of the groundbreaking project proposals that my dad had submitted to his company, and he rose rapidly to a managerial position, until the effects of the Great Depression began to hit Southern Africa. Businesses everywhere ground to a halt. The only work my dad could find was in the Rhodesia Railways, and that was where he stayed until he retired. His drinking led to appalling conditions within our home. My respect for him dissipated. Actually, I never really knew him. When I got up for school, he was still sleeping; and when I went to bed, he was not yet home. When I was fifteen, I was the same height as him and told him that if he ever laid a hand on my mother again, I was going to beat him up. He never abused her again.

My dad kicked me out of our home when I was seventeen because I had become a disciple of Jesus Christ. I found refuge in the home of my close friend, Doug Roberts, who went on to become one of South Africa's leading architects. His parents, Claude and Theresa, became my spiritual parents, and I am forever grateful for the way they loved and discipled me. My mother pleaded with my dad to let me return home, but he was adamant, until she announced that she was also leaving. I was allowed home, and a crude truce clicked in.

Dad's alcoholism never interfered with his job, but it persisted until at the age of fifty-two, when he suffered two massive heart attacks. The doctor told him that if he went on drinking, the next attack would take his life. He went to Alcoholics Anonymous for help, but the man assigned to help my dad was weak-willed; and before the evening was up, they were both drunk. This did not endear AA to my dad, and when my wife and I and our four children arrived from Zambia en route to a coastal holiday, my dad was desperate and came to me for help. I had training and some experience in counseling alcoholics but was extremely nervous about taking on my dad. I remembered that there was a man in our church in Salisbury (now Harare) who had an engineering background, had been an alcoholic, and somehow had been converted. I phoned him up, and yes, he would be prepared to listen to my dad. I dropped Dad there at 7:00 p.m. and picked him up just after 10:00 p.m. Dad had repented and handed his life over to the Lord. Was it real? Did it last?

Dad lived another ten years. He and my mother had the best years of their marriage. They became faithful members in our church. Dad never had another drink, and when he died, we all gathered to honor the memory of a generous, gentle man, a man who, by God's grace, overcame a cruel addiction and became the answer to more than twenty years of prayer. Once famous in almost every bar in Rhodesia, he became known for a quiet spirit and real self-control. Our one regret was that, as busy missionaries, we did not question my dad on how he managed to go cold turkey from excess in drinking to total abstinence. As I work with addicts today, they all ask that question.

My Mother

My mother, Elizabeth Jessie Speed Robertson Comrie was born in Dundee, Scotland, and grew up with her mum and dad and older brother, Bill, in a modest home. Her home became dysfunctional after they immigrated to Rhodesia, and her dad became a prodigal who wheeled and dealed, wined and dined in society in Johannesburg.

Mum was a nurse and a midwife, who, after marriage to my dad, nursed in Bloemfontein where my dad was working for the Vacuum Oil Company of South Africa. That was Heather's birthplace. Mum's story of the ugly effects of the Great Depression were graphic. Dad was one of thousands who lost their jobs and then headed up to Bulawayo in Rhodesia, finding work on the Rhodesia Railways. Mum rode her bike, first to the Lady Rodwell in Bulawayo, where she worked and where I was born. When Dad was transferred to Salisbury, she rode her bike to Salisbury General Hospital, where, a little later, Sheila was born.

Mum was great fun. Along with Granny, she brought us up, loved us, spanked us, and shielded us from the negative influences of an alcoholic father. She introduced me to tennis, which quickly became my focus (more about that later). Mum nearly died a few times from malaria, blackwater fever, and hepatitis. I can remember, as a little boy, kneeling beside her bed and pleading with her not to die. Granny was weeping in the background. Thankfully, her life was spared. Mum showed little emotion when I became a Christian, until Dad ejected me from the home. For five weeks, she interceded with Dad on my behalf; but as you have already learned, it was not until she took drastic action that I was reluctantly allowed to return. We had loose connections with the Presbyterian Church but never attended as a family. I did go to Boy's Brigade.

During the war, Scottish international football players were sent to Rhodesia for their protection. We benefitted from their coaching, and nine of the Mashonaland Under-14 team came from our Boy's Brigade. It was my privilege to be one of them. I realized later what a sham that was. Fancy playing for Mashonaland without one Shona-speaking person on the team! Mum took little interest in our Christian commitment, but when Gwyn and I announced that God had fine-tuned our call into full-time ministry and that we were heading as a family into missionary work in Northern Rhodesia (now Zambia), she was galvanized into action and arranged a meeting with the minister of our home church. He agreed with her that we were making a terrible mistake. He wrote to us, saying that with all the training we had, we were overqualified for missions but had the appropriate training for the pastoral ministry. I respectfully replied that while I had the minimum qualifications for pastoral ministry, I was underqualified for missionary service and would seek continual upgrading. It took that minister fifteen years to apologize for that letter, but he eventually did and agreed that cross-cultural, multilingual ministry carried greater challenge and danger. His local church flourished as it became global in its outreach and influence.

In 1966, Mum came to visit us at Chizera Bible Institute in Zambia. She had refused the invitation so many times that it seemed unbelievable. We had shown her to the guest room and left her to unpack. Andrew, our second son, was just three and remained with her. Lifting the bedcover and looking under the bed, he suddenly shouted, "Snake, snake!" A few days before, a full-grown cobra had found its way into that room, which forced us to tell Mum the story. Doug, our five-year-old, had come rushing home the previous week in time for supper, missed the wooden part of the frame on our verandah door, and pushed a hole through the rotting gauze wire. I did not fix it immediately, and it became the entry point for the cobra. I had read that if your dog (we had a German shepherd) went up on the tips of his toes like a frightened ballet dancer, it meant that there was a snake present, but the dog could not locate it. So as soon as I heard Doug's shout, I yelled for help.

One of our students, Fainoti Kalubenyi, was near and came running. He fetched his spear, and we began a systematic search. We had suitable weapons to use when the snake showed itself. We started in the guest room but discovered the snake was behind a cupboard in the closed-in verandah in the adjoining the room. Fainoti used a pole to tip up the cupboard, and as he put the spear on the floor, I aimed just behind the head and slid the spear with force toward the snake.

The spear sliced into the snake, and the cobra came out from his hiding place. The venom missed my eye but sprayed down my cheek and neck. The skin was discolored for days. Our weapons did their work, and we hung the seven-foot cobra over the washing line and lectured the crowd that gathered on the fearsome poison that snake carried. It was estimated at that time that cobras were responsible for twenty-five thousand deaths every year in Africa alone.

After a few hiccups, Mum settled in and began to meet the people and see the work. The clinic was run by Gwyneth, who, like my mother, was a trained nurse and midwife. It was more than exciting as she had plenty of hands-on experience. Mum's spiritual perceptions were sharpened as she came to a full understanding of what it meant to have a relationship with the living God. After a few weeks, she returned to Rhodesia to become one of our strongest advocates and supporters.

My Other Sister

I have already told the remarkable story of my younger sister, Sheila, and the encouraging fruit from her tragic murder.

Heather is my older sister. I have already mentioned her ability as a dancer and the amazing privilege she had of dancing before the king, queen, and princesses in 1947 during their royal visit to Rhodesia. Heather inherited my dad's scriptwriting ability and became a meticulous bookkeeper, ending up working for twenty-seven years for a firm of civil engineers in Salisbury.

Heather was beautiful and great fun. Her admirers multiplied until Brian McKay, the son of a South African judge and his wife, arrived in Salisbury and swept Heather off her feet. They made a handsome couple and were married when Heather was only seventeen. I was fifteen at their wedding, but no one questioned my right to fully participate in the champagne that flowed so freely. Having observed all the negative effects of having an alcoholic father, I had determined in my own mind and promised my mother that I would never be deceived by strong drinks. I can remember my mother's wail as I was carried, hopelessly drunk, from that reception. What kept me from continuing excess was my position as one of Rhodesia's up-and-coming young tennis players. My coach Bill Clements was famous as the number two squash player in the world, and he wrote in our *Daily Herald* that I could become one of the youngest players to get to Wimbledon. I learned that if you wanted to excel, you had to be single-minded and totally committed. and for those teen years, I was in boots and all!

Ian was born to Brian and Heather, and there was a definite plan for more children. Brian was my idea of what a man should be. Tall, good-looking, first-team rugby, a prefect, an honors student, and he owned an MG TC! My brother-in-law was my mentor, who, for five years, loved Heather to the fullest until the accident. Like everyone else, he had to complete his army training. On one call up for service, he was riding in the back of an army truck on a hot day in October. In the back of the truck were two forty-four-gallon drums of petrol. For some reason, a soldier opened one of the drums to fill his lighter. Petrol fumes poured out just as Brian in the back of the truck was lighting up a cigarette. Immediately, he became a human torch, mesmerizing those who were looking on. He fell out the back, and finally, a man jumped down and put out the flames with an army greatcoat and a blanket. If Brian had died, it would have been merciful. His ears and nose were 90 percent burnt off, and third-degree burns covered most of his body. He never shaved again.

My wife-to-be, Gwyn Payne, was one of the nursing sisters on the ward where Brian was being treated. She remembered Heather as a beautiful wife who almost lived at the hospital. Months of skin grafting and pain would follow. The good-looking Brian McKay, in spite of all the grafting, was grotesquely scarred, not only on his body but in his mind. Neither his parents, his wife, nor any of the medical community could even begin to counsel or reason with him. He became angry, violent, and rebellious. His rage was fueled by alcohol. He threatened not only Heather's existence but also that of their son, Ian. Fearing her harm, Heather was advised to flee the man she loved. The marriage I had called ideal was shattered. Brian became a bum on First Street, Salisbury, and was often in trouble with the law. He fled to his native South Africa, where we heard he died in his late thirties.

After I was called into Christian ministry, the dark clouds of Brian's tragedy and pain galvanized me in the study of biblical counseling principles that would aid in similar situations. There are no pat answers, but there are growing numbers from similar afflictions and addictions that bear witness to the healing and wholeness they are receiving in relationship with the Lord Jesus Christ. I still dream that somewhere on his lonely, bewildering journey, Brian could have met someone who could have understood his pain and who could have led him to the only One able to bring the healing and forgiveness that he needed.

In her third marriage to Sandy Stephenson, Heather had two more sons, David and Sean. They both swam for Rhodesia in their age-group before tragedy struck once again. A car hit David as he was trying desperately to keep up with his stepbrother, Ian, on their way to a soccer match; they were trying to cross Jameson Avenue (now Samora Machel) in Harare. He was unconscious for months. When he came to, he was only slightly handicapped, but enough to affect his schooling and ultimately for him to have a sheltered home and workplace. At one stage of desperation, David decided to end it all by jumping in front of a bus. The surgeons saved his life but had to amputate his leg.

The unmistakable hand of God was there reaching out to David. He became an incredibly brave man as he found real peace and forgiveness in a personal relationship with Jesus Christ. Patience and kindness too grew as he navigated his wheelchair into the rooms and then into hearts of many of his fellow sufferers.

Toward the end of her life, Heather developed chronic emphysema. Her marriage with Sandy had broken, and she was living alone in Avondale in Salisbury. My wife and I were living in Salisbury but ministering in fourteen countries. Life was hectic, but in between countries, we gave priority to Heather, visiting her daily. She was a quiet, respectful listener as we talked of our faith and love for the Lord, but she remained totally uncommitted. One of our morning visits revealed just how hard it was for her to breathe even with a constant supply of oxygen. That afternoon, I was driving past her home after another appointment. There was no voice but a strong conviction that I needed to see her again. As I went in, she did not greet me but called out, "Roy, I know that you have always wanted me to become a Christian, but it is not fair! I have lived my life, have made bad choices, failed in three marriages, and now when I am about to die…it is just not fair!" After the breathlessness of the morning, where did she get the strength to call out that long sentence?

"You are right, Heather. It's not fair, but it is God's undeserved favor offered to us in the face of our rebellion."

I remembered that Jesus had quoted these very words in His parable to the workers (Matthew 20). I told Heather the story. Workers came at different times of the day, but all agreed on the same wage. When the time came to be paid, the ones who had worked the whole day commented on the unfairness, "You have made them equal to us, who have borne the burden of the work and the heat of the day." The reply was profound: "Friend, I am not being unfair to you. Didn't you agree to work for a denarius? Take your pay and go. I want to give the man who was hired last the same as you. Don't I have the right to do what I want with my own money? Or are you envious because I am generous?"

The answer Jesus gave opened a window of light and truth in Heather's heart. Not wanting to push her too hard, I gave her a booklet, *Finding God* by Frank Retief. When I arrived next morning, Heather was like a morning glory flower, opening to the sunshine of God's love in Christ. Her prayer of repentance and faith told the story of sins forgiven, settled peace, and relationship with God. She died two days later. It was my privilege and challenge to conduct her funeral on the Friday of that week. Every member of her firm of civil engineers was present. Did they or some members of our extended family and friends even believe the story I told of Heather's journey to faith? Some who expressed doubt told me about it when they came to faith years later. Heather's husband Sandy became a believer, as did her three sons Ian, David, and Sean. How great and merciful is our God!

Chapter 3

MY CONVERSION
AND CALL

Sheila's influence in my life was profound. It was not her persuasiveness but her changed life that tipped the scale. I had to go through her room to get to the rest of our house. She was either reading her Bible or praying. Her invitations were urgent, and the joy in her life and those of her girlfriends was compelling. I had to take a closer look! That took me to Young People's on a Friday night and the Sunday evening service. I went armed to defend my unbelief. The minister, Sydney Hudson Reed, seemed to have been expecting me and asked for a game of tennis during the week. I was horrified. How could this old (he was thirty-four, exactly double my age) prelate possibly keep up with someone who was hoping to be playing at Wimbledon the following year? He was tenacious, and three weeks later, we walked onto the court together. Though I beat him easily, I could see that he had a background in the game and learned that he had played at provincial level in his younger days. When he asked what kept me from faith, I told him that the Bible was full of contradictions and that the church was full of hypocrites.

"Oh," he said, "you have read the Bible."

"No," I said. "It's so flawed. That was not necessary."

"I will agree," he said, "that we have a number of hypocrites in the church, but that is dealt with when they come to faith." After establishing the fact that I had a Bible, he said, "Tell you what, you start reading in the New Testament, mark the contradictions, and we will discuss them."

I thought that I would have a pile of them in no time and started reading in Matthew. I found difficulties but no contradictions, and I was amazed that the Word seemed to know me so well. When I listened to Syd preaching, I was sure he had obtained information about me from Sheila, which happened when David Evans preached too. When Sheila was to be baptized, I invited a group of my unbelieving friends to come for a laugh when they put Sheila right under the water. Before the baptism, Syd preached on John 14:6: "I am the way the truth and the life. No one comes to the Father but by me." If what Jesus said was true, I was in deep trouble. None of us were laughing. I knew that Jesus was who He claimed to be. My readings had taken me through the Gospel of Matthew to Mark 8:36: "What good is it for a man to gain the whole world yet forfeit his soul?"

My whole world was tennis, so what if I went all the way yet forfeited my own soul? The pieces all began to fall into place. I was a sinner and needed a Savior. I repented and begged for His forgiveness. I was born from above and became part of the family of God. Somehow I knew from that very first day that I would love Him and serve Him for the rest of my life. How utterly unworthy I was, and am, but "if anyone is in Christ Jesus, he is a new creation, old things are passed away, all things have become new." Could it be that I was called to serve Him the day I received His salvation?

That certainly was the beginning, but in His mercy, the Lord confirmed that calling three more times. First in 1955, when Dr. Oswald J Smith came from People's Church in Toronto, Canada, to our church in Salisbury (Harare). He spoke eight days in a row, Sunday to Sunday, on *The Man God Uses*, the title of one of his books. To begin with, I had a negative reaction, thinking him proud and boastful. I was wrong. He was a humble, holy man of God from a different culture. His passion for the Savior and vision for the world shone out. Fourteen of us responded to his invitation to serve the Lord full-time. Forty-seven years later, all fourteen were still serving. My future wife, Gwyneth Payne, was one of those who responded.

The second confirmation of my call came in 1961, a year after our wedding, when I attended the Urbana student missionary conference at the University of Illinois in Chicago. Festo Kivengere from Uganda was the main speaker. I can repeat now almost verbatim the message he gave on Jacob and Esau. It was on the lordship of Christ in missions. The week after I got back to Toronto, where I was the part-time associate pastor in our High Park Church, I preached and reported, mentioning that God had given us 2 Timothy 2:2: "The things that you have heard from me…commit to faithful men and women, who will be able to teach others also." We could see ourselves in missions in a training role, preparing others for service. After the service, a group including the director for Canada of the South Africa General Mission, which later became the Africa Evangelical Fellowship, Peter Letchford, surrounded us. He listened to the conversation and went home and, that night, wrote a five-page letter outlining the possibilities for a couple to fill a vacancy in Nyasaland (Malawi) or Northern Rhodesia (Zambia).

The third confirmation came at our seminary missions retreat soon after this. God moved mightily, and a senior group of graduates volunteered for missions in Japan, India, and Africa. We decided that as we were not Canadians, it would be wrong to raise support in Canada. We were allowed to join the Canadian branch of our mission, and they agreed that we should find our support in our own churches in Rhodesia. That meant that we could leave quickly. But just before we were due to sail, in one week, we got invitations from three churches to become their pastor. It was confusing. We wrote the same letter to each church, thanking them for the honor of being invited but telling them of the conviction we had from the Lord that it was to be missions. We told them that we would pray for them as they searched for the right man. All three replied quickly to say that if we could not come as their pastor, they would delight to support us as missionaries. We got our full support from them, and fifty years later, they were still supporting us. How great is our God! When we got to Africa, our churches said they could not support us as we had joined an interdenominational mission, and their policy was Baptist money for Baptist missions. In time, they changed their policy, but our base in Canada was established. In 1962, Gwyn and I with one son, Douglas, set sail for Africa, then on to Chizera Bible Institute in Northern Rhodesia. They got independence in 1964 when the name was changed to Zambia. What a privilege to train people who came to us from five different countries.

Some Background at Rhodes University

When I realized that God was calling me to full-time service, I got cold feet. Maybe a university degree would convince me that there were many ways in which I could serve the Lord. Like Jonah, I was on the run. Like Jonah, I was running the wrong way. How kind of the Lord to bring me to the end of myself, to the point that I could once again discern the Shepherd's voice. Tennis took front and center again. InterVarsity was coming up, and I was told that if I could beat the guys above me on the ladder, I would automatically make the team. I climbed to the number two position, imagining that I would be secure. I was wrong. Some seniors, knowing that it was their last year, got together and wrongly reported the results. When the team was announced and I was not on it, I went to see the captain, Owen Emslie. Deep in his heart, I think he knew what had happened, but it was their word against mine. I wrote in my daily reading, "Surely, Lord, the best should go!" I wept at the omission. My attempt to resurrect my tennis world was backfiring.

The Rhodes tennis championships were coming up. I trained hard, and it was difficult not to think of revenge. Owen Emslie asked me to partner him in the men's doubles, and I carefully chose a partner for the mixed doubles. I was sure I could make it to the singles final as Owen was in the other half of the draw. He was a provincial player knocking on the South African door, and I gauged that he would be too much for me. In the kindness of the Lord, Owen faltered, and the final went to a final set. After the humiliation of InterVarsity, I won all three titles, and the press had a heyday. The headlines in Eastern Province and in Rhodesia (Zimbabwe) were, "RED FACES AT RHODES." Lies work for a while, but the truth will come out. That, for me, was a lesson for life. The battle for truth still rages on. God is never late, but patience is required while His truth is worked out. Too often I had been impatient.

When John Stott, the Anglican minister from All Souls, Langham Place, in London came on a mission to Rhodes University, the fresh winds of revival swept through. My cold heart was set alight, and through discourse and debate, I saw that the gospel is the power of God for salvation to everyone who will believe, and I could hardly wait to prepare myself in earnest to become one of His servants and ambassadors. The following year, when I moved to Johannesburg for theological training, John Stott arrived to take a mission at Wits University. The great hall at Wits was packed, and every student from our college was also present.

While John was speaking, the atheist society of Wits decided to placard his meeting. They walked silently down the aisles with huge placards proclaiming their atheism. One said, "You lie, you lie, there is no God." When there was no reaction to their silent protest, they began to shout out their message. John invited their chairman to come and use the microphone to air their grievance. The chairman chided the whole congregation for their ignorance in allowing a faith-based movement to speak to people who were sup-posed to be intellectuals. He challenged John Stott to a debate on the existence of God. John accepted, and the Saturday was named as the date. Professors and students alike were on tiptoe, and the great hall definitely broke every fire regulation. The rules of debate were carefully followed. The brilliant young student chairman was no novice to debate. His carefully constructed argument had seven-teen points. I took them all down and wondered why John was not writing furiously. To all of our amazement, John graciously and in order answered each point and powerfully presented the apologetics for the existence of God. At the end of that very long evening, to the glory of God, that young student came to faith in Christ. The atheist society at Wits was disbanded. The year was 1958. Its history shows that, twenty years later, there was still no atheist society.

The Professor of Old Testament at Rhodes University in 1957 was a young man called Dr. William Kosser. Because of my interest, I audited his course. It was a wake-up call for me. He did not believe in miracles, the virgin birth, or the resurrection. He went fishing every Sunday, and he fell in love with one of the senior female students in his class. She was beautiful and intelligent. A lot of the single guys were looking longingly in her direction! They were very discreet, and nobody knew of the relationship. It did not take Dr. Kosser long, and he decided that this was the girl for him, and he proposed. She was bowled over by the interest of the professor but politely turned down his proposal. When he questioned her, she said she would not marry a non-Christian.

"What do you mean?" he said. "I am the professor of Old Testament at Rhodes University."

"Yes," she said, "but you are not a believer. You have never been born again like Nicodemus in John 3."

Dr. Kosser took a sabbatical and went to European universities to search out the question of the new birth. They all backed his assertion that the new birth was irrelevant until, in one university, he met a professor who was a believer and led him to faith in the finished work of Christ. I was not at Rhodes when Dr. Kosser returned, but I heard that he was a transformed teacher and eventually married the young lady who had jolted him into action.

InterVarsity Fellowship at Rhodes was galvanized into action when the Lord moved so mightily during the John Stott mission. Teams of students were sent and literally took over local churches in East London and Port Elizabeth. I was privileged to be part of the East London teams. There was not room for two of us in the cars going, so they took our entire luggage, and we hitchhiked. For hours, we waited at the rendezvous. The car with our luggage was involved in an accident. We had no address or money, and they had no smartphone to let us know. Late that night, the police questioned us. We ended up in a downtown cell. It was all settled the next day, and we had a story to tell. Strangely enough, I was preaching in that same church in January of this year (2016), and there were folk who remembered that event from 1957. What God did that weekend through our enthusiastic student ministry helped me realize that full-time ministry was indeed His call for me.

Our Love Story

At the age of sixteen, before I met the Lord, I found myself in a lineup at Amanzimtoti Beach on the south coast of South Africa with a R10.00 note to have sex with an underage girl. The guys described her as great. First thoughts were, I'd become a man. I tried to convince myself she was just a thing, not a person. She was underage, well, so was I. Lust had to be fulfilled. Will love wait? I became confused and saw the whole thing as cheating and cheap and left the line. When I turned to the Lord the next year, God brought a beautiful young lady into my life, and I learned about love and respect and that sex is a lovely gift reserved for marriage. We got very serious and spoke of marriage. I was going to Rhodes University to major in English and physical education; Jenny was going to a teachers' college in the same city. Then came my call up to the army, no debate there. We wrote every day. Then came the "Dear Roy." My heart was shattered. When I met Alex Borraine, I had to agree that Jenny had chosen a great man. He eventually became the leading figure, along with Bishop Tutu, in the Truth and Reconciliation program in South Africa after Nelson Mandela came to power.

I never thought there would be anyone to measure up to Jenny. I was wrong. My roommate Clayton at college was from Pretoria and wanted to get to know a girl in our church in Salisbury (Harare). The girl, Gwyneth, had a sister called Iris. I made the arrangement during this short break for the four of us to get together each day. I noticed that Clayton was not doing well with Gwyneth. My appreciation for Gwyn was growing by the hour, but I dared not say anything that would distract from Clayton's declared desire. Clayton had no breakthrough and actually left early to return to his home in Pretoria. I could no longer use Clayton as my excuse for seeing Gwyn, and my friends reminded me that she was three years older than me and was probably looking up, not down.

Time came for Gwyn and a dozen others to go back to Bible Institute at Kalk Bay in Cape Town. About a hundred people came to say good-bye to them at the railway station. I felt very small and insignificant, but I was totally focused on this lovely lady. Everybody had to say good-bye to everybody, and it all seemed so inadequate. When Gwyn got on the train, I caught her eye and held it as the train slowly picked up speed. Our eyes never lost focus until the train rounded a bend.

I went home and told my mum that I now knew whom I was going to marry.

"Who?" she asked.

"Gwyneth," I said.

"Dinna be daft" (Scottish for "you're crazy"). "She is not looking at your age-grouping."

When I told her of the eye contact, she quieted down. We began to exchange letters—me, Gwyn, and Clayton. Really romantic! Strangely enough, we were both (Gwyn and I) praying that if God was in this, without our organizing it, we would somehow be together on the next short vacation. Our letters crossed, I wrote, "I have been asked to be a counselor at a boys' camp in Port Elizabeth." She wrote, "I have been asked to be a counselor at a girls' camp in Carmel in George." I rushed for the Atlas. How far was it between Port Elizabeth and George? My heart sank. Any contact would have been impossible. The distance was too great. Was this just an impossible dream? Hard to hold on to hope in those circumstances.

The night before I was to leave for Port Elizabeth, I got a phone call from the director. "We have not received enough applications from boys, so we have decided to move the whole camp over to Carmel in George to be together with the girls' camp. Go straight to Carmel!"

I did not have time to get in touch with Gwyn. I was so excited and filled with praise. Never will I forget the look in Gwyn's eyes when I walked in on her at Carmel. We went for an amazing walk, confessed our love, and got unofficially engaged. Talk about the unmistakable hand of God. Nearly fifty-seven years later, our marriage is strong, tender, and true. I remember one person saying that it was just coincidence and that there were at least twenty other ladies whom I could have met and married and written that it was God's leading. My conviction in writing this book tells why it is incumbent upon us to trace His hand so that we can give Him all the glory for His specific choice.

After Gwyn had accepted my proposal, she told me that she wanted a three-diamond ring, with one large diamond and two smaller ones the same size. The large diamond was to signify the Lord as a Sovereign Shepherd, and the smaller ones would represent us. As a penniless student, one diamond would have constituted a miracle! When she got home, her mother said, "I have never told you, but when your grandmother died, she left a five-diamond ring. Three stones were for you, and two for Iris." The sizes were perfect. A tennis, friend of mine who was also a jeweler charged me twelve pounds and ten shillings to put the diamonds and gold ring together, and by the grace of God, we got officially engaged. Having entered college single, the rule was that I could not get married until I graduated over two years later. I reminded myself of Jacob and stopped complaining. After four years of nurses' training and two years of Bible Institute, Gwyn ended up in Johannesburg for her midwifery training. The Old Vic was just around the corner from our college. Between us, we had bought a side-valve Morris Minor; and though we were both hectically busy, we managed some magical moments at the Wilds, a park nearby.

Our principal, Dr. Charles Stern, and his wife fell in love with Gwyn and gave us some special care. Supremely a man of prayer, Dr. Stern said he could not get us out of his mind and, one day toward the end of that year, shared the following request. He had pastored a church in Canada and taught in the seminary there. Would we consider completing our third and fourth years in Canada? The program in South Africa was based on that of Canada, and I would get full credit for what I had done. He said that as both of us had never left the shores of Africa, it would give us the opportunity of seeing our continent from afar and sorting through some of the cultural and racial issues. Wise counsel indeed. The bonus was that we could start planning for our wedding. So began our Canada connection.

My best friend all through high school was Walter Garrett. We agreed that we would both go into the air force. We both applied and passed all initial testing. Then I was offered a scholarship to go to university. The air force said I should complete my degree first then reapply. So I prepared to go to Rhodes, and Walter went straight into the air force. The week he was to get his wings, he was flying the Hawker Hunter in formation with two others and got caught in their slipstream. He was given full military honors. My heart was broken. Death appeared to me as a robber. I wept unashamedly. It was the beginning for me of processing the real meaning of the death of Christ, which eventually led to my conversion.

When Gwyn and I were to be married, Walter's parents offered to give us our reception as a gift in memory of their son. In the center of Salisbury City Park, the most attractive wedding reception venue in the country was the restaurant owned by them. The surrounding gardens and a beautiful day of sunshine propelled everyone into thanksgiving for the generosity of the parents, who really loved the Lord, and the memory of such a great pal. As penniless students, we traced the hand of Jehovah Jireh, our Provider.

Chapter 4

MISSIONARY SERVICE BEGINS

A Remarkable Man of God

He was almost old enough to be my father when we arrived at Chizera, Zambia, in 1962. Tall and wiry with a steady eye, he loved the Lord deeply and communicated him effectively. He was my counselor and my friend. Our relationship was cemented when I preached in his church and in his language just three months after arriving in Zambia.

We did so much together: evangelism and church planting, pastoral visitation, and praying for the sick and those grossly affected by the demonic.

His name was Pastor Nenechi Bonshe, a true man of God and an outstanding man of prayer. In all our travels, sleeping in the same mud hut or room, he would awake at about 4:00 a.m., and he always prayed aloud. Often, I would just lie in the dark and listen to him. He knew the Lord intimately and walked with him in every area of his life.

We hunted and fished together. I have never met a better tracker and stalker. We were in a tsetse-fly area where cattle and pigs could not survive. The nearest butcher was over four hundred kilometers away, but we lived in a superabundant wild-game area. Allowances for hunting were generous, so we rejoiced in God's ample supply for the ten years of our stay.

One day, as we walked through the bush looking for meat for an upcoming church conference, we met a huge male lion and four lionesses. We were walking single file, Pastor Nenechi leading, me right behind him, and four other nationals bringing up the rear. The lions were just twenty to twenty-five meters ahead of us. My heart was pounding against my chest. Pastor Nenechi was very calm. "Just stand very still," he said. "They know where we are, and like any cat, we must never give them anything to chase." He later told me that lions always prefer wild to human flesh, until they get old and tooth-less, and then they may become man-eaters.

This pride of five was in the prime of life. At least two lionesses were pregnant. Exactly as Pastor Nenechi predicted, after keeping us waiting for what seemed like an age (perhaps it was as much as four minutes), one lioness went slowly off, followed one by one by the others. None of them gave us a second glance. We, fortunately, did not even amount to a meal. All the delicacies were ahead of them, and they were all on four legs!

Later that same day, the human side of Pastor Nenechi, with a lesson in their cultural understanding during colonial days, emerged. We began to doubt any supply of meat for our church conference when suddenly we came on a small group of antelopes called puku. The colonial government law said we could only shoot a male, and we could see only four females. When I refused to shoot a female, Pastor Nenechi got angry with me and quickly took off his shirt, loaded his muzzle-loader gun, which dated back to the 19th century, and began a puzzling yet brilliant stalk on the open plain. When he raised his ancient weapon, he was no more than five meters from his chosen target.

As we gathered around the dead animal, his first words were *tulombe* (let's pray). "Lord, this morning, early, we asked you to guide us and to protect us in our hunt for meat for our church conference. You have protected us from the lions, and you brought this animal right across our path at the end of this day. We thank you for this blessing for all your people who will come to the conference." For him, the need for food took precedent over the law!

We had many discussions about this principle, and though he understood our position as foreigners in his land, he never ever applied it when faced with the needs of the poor, the local people, in the wilds of Africa.

Fire!

The conference was called *Kipwilo kya Kisalo* (the dry-season gathering). We had meat, and there was great expectation of blessing. Gray Watson's dad, Mr. Percy Watson (I never heard anyone ever calling him Percy; it was always Mr. Watson), a veteran from our pioneer work in Angola, was the guest speaker. He and his wife had moved to Luampa in Zambia to reach the Angolans who had settled there after their country had exploded in civil war, resulting from Marxist expansionism into that part of the world, a selfish grab for the diamonds and the oil.

Everybody slept in a temporary individual family shelter made from trees and elephant grass. Our shelter was next to Mr. Watson's. On the Saturday night, Mr. Watson was sitting on his grass mattress, preparing for Sunday with the aid of kerosene or what we called a paraffin lantern. As he fell asleep, he knocked over the lantern, and the dry grass ignited. We had just put out our lantern to retire for the night when we saw the flame. I put a blanket over my head and rushed into the burning shelter. I grabbed Mr. Watson and dragged him in a rather undignified manner out of the burning shelter.

Bewildered and terrified, he kept yelling, "My Bible! My Bible! Go back in there! Get my Bible!"

Without thinking, I pulled the blanket back over my head and body and attempted to get in, but to no avail. People emerged from their shelters and from the surrounding villages, and a great crowd watched as Mr. Watson's shelter with his suitcase and all he had brought with him burned to a cinder. When the fire had burned itself out, I went back into his devastated shelter, and there, miraculously, lying on a portion of very dry grass, was his open Bible. I used both hands to carry it out. It was open at the passage, "Heaven and earth shall pass away but my word will never pass away" (Matthew 24:35). Mr. Watson, with a little encouragement from Pastor Nenechi, felt a sermon coming on. The message penetrated the darkness of many hearts that night, resulting in transformed lives, and it was still being spoken of thirty years later.

Children Challenges and Blessings

Andrew was not yet two, sitting in his sandbox and flicking sand at something. Doug was four, sitting near the sandbox on a chair, enduring a haircut from me (I used the old-fashioned clippers). Suddenly it came into focus: the object of Andrew's interest was a full-grown boomslang ("tree snake"). Back-fanged, there was no cure for its bite. In panic, I ran inside and picked up my shotgun. Andrew was partially in front of it, and any shot would have been dangerous and terrifying. My decisiveness was blocked, and suddenly the snake came straight for me, or so I thought. I was standing next to a large tree. Though I took a swing at the snake with my gun, I missed it, and it sped up the tree and stopped when it was in the topmost branches. I shot it, and the SSG cut the boomslang in half about ten inches behind its head. Seven feet of snake was left up in the tree, and the ten inches fell down.

Immediately my German shepherd rushed in and swallowed the head. All our concern now turned to the dog. Surely, a fang would penetrate, and the poison be released. He lay there quietly unconcerned until suddenly he began to retch. Up came the whole ten inches of snake. He went back to the shade until the other seven feet of snake was released from the top branches and fell right between us—harmless, of course—but it sure got the adrenaline going. We scooped up Andrew and thought of the might-have-beens. There was much thanksgiving that night.

Our now two-and-a-half-year-old Andrew was very excited. He came running into our home at Chizera holding a full-grown scorpion, the one with the thick tail, which was the most venomous. Not lethal to an adult, they will take you through some of the worst pain you have ever felt; but with little children, there is a 20 percent chance of it being fatal. I smacked his hand, and the scorpion went flying, and my boot came down on it before it could move. Andrew looked at me in horror. This was his insect friend. I put him on my lap and explained the ugliness of the owie he had escaped and apologized for my seeming brutality.

Our daughter, Janice, was nine when she had a sleepover with her friend. She wondered why she was put in a separate room but was wakened by the father of the house. She liked him because he played with them. That was a blind to practice his deviant behavior. There was no penetration, but she was sexually abused and then threatened. This was going to be their secret; if she told us, he said that we would not be allowed to stay in the country as missionaries. As parents, we never guessed. We thought that with rockets and mortars landing, fearfulness filled Jan's heart; however, the little girl who used to cuddle up to me as I read to her suddenly pulled away when I approached. I imagined that a time would come when she became a young lady that there would be some change, but this seemed premature. I realize now what an immature parent I was and too overwhelmingly busy to push for any answers. However, we were praying, and God, in His mercy, stepped in. the abuser was called up for army duty and was killed on the front line. I only know that in the depths of my thoughts, I could easily have been arrested for murder. As you all know, when my sister Sheila was murdered, God gave me, first, the desire then the opportunity to forgive the guilty man. His grace only comes when we need it.

Janice totally blocked out the memory of this episode and never went back to that house. Until Janice dealt with this years later with friends praying for her, that memory surfaced again, and she found real deliverance. Her experienced freedom enables her to help and counsel so many bound by the same or similar issues today.

Without a Christian model of discipline, as a young husband and father, I failed my first two children. When, in their anguish, they pointed this out to me years later, God gave me the understanding I needed and enabled me to ask for their forgiveness. They forgave me, and our relationship was restored. Some have questioned my attitude, saying that the children would lose respect. Forgiveness is not a beggar's refuge but a Christian's privilege. The fact is, this brought us closer than ever.

It is possible to forgive too soon. Paul's injunction in 1 Corinthians 5:1–5, in this case of gross immorality, sounds unforgiving, but notice the purpose clause in verse 5: "Hand this man over to Satan, so that the sinful nature may be destroyed and his spirit saved on the day of the Lord." If we forgive too soon, the lesson may not be learned, and the last state will be worse than the first. That should lead to a good discussion.

On a lighter note, walking through the bush near Chizeia one day, we came upon a baby duiker. It was hiding in a thicket. A mother duiker will never leave her baby, so we decided that she had met a dreadful fate, maybe a predator or a hunter. If you think it's easy to run down a tiny little duiker on what looked like matchstick legs, think again! Two of us ran for about two kilometers before Antonyo managed to trip it up, and I held it gently but firmly.

Gwyn and Bruce (our youngest) and Mark Frew 1

As we searched for the right formula, it had diarrhea for almost three months but finally became strong. It became what our children called the best pet ever. The word *Bambi* was used, but mostly it was baby duiker. It was never caged and had the same freedom as our dog, which loved and protected it. Her eyes were like deep pools, and as you can see from the picture, she kept the attention of all of us. Every visitor was intrigued with her beauty, and people around the world wanted an update on her health. Her speeding across our parklike property and then stopping abruptly was entertaining.

We realized that she was full-grown when she left our property. When she came back, we realized that she was pregnant. We had occasional visits and realized there was a male more important than us. Then she left for what we thought was for good, but weeks later, she came back with her baby. We made one mistake: in the joy of it all, we did not get a picture of them together. We never saw her again. We had the fulfillment of every animal lover's dream. The lady had her priorities, and her family and husband came before us as pet owners. We felt privileged and content to take our place in the order of things.

Chapter 5

THE DEADLIEST OF ALL SNAKEBITES

My four-wheel long-drive wheelbase Willys Jeep was ideal for the rough road leading to the Kalengwa Open Cast copper mine. Newly opened, they were excited about the prospect of harvesting copper, which was reckoned to be the highest grade of any ever mined anywhere. A new road was proposed that would more quickly deliver this bounty to the copper belt of Zambia, about four hundred kilometers away. This trip was a bit of an emergency as our much-loved German shepherd dog had developed sleeping sickness, and I knew from previous trips that the mine administration kept a stock of the medication needed.

One of the senior students of the Bible Institute, Fainoti Kalubenyi, was with me and was excitedly pointing out the great variety of wildlife that populated this area. It was better than any game park that I had visited. Suddenly, lying across the road on a bend was Africa's most feared snake, the black mamba. As we barreled toward it, it reared. Its head was higher than the Jeep. It is considered the fastest snake in the world and the deadliest in Africa, and when threatened, it puts on an awesome display. As we drew alongside it, it struck my windshield. Although we were perfectly safe, instinctively, Fainoti and I ducked and bumped heads. We laughed at our own foolishness and looked back to see the four-meter snake going very slowly into the bush.

Growing up in Africa, once on the Zambezi Valley of Zimbabwe and once in the Mufumbwe in Zambia, we saw a full-grown mamba traveling at speed with its head two meters from the ground. On the Mufumbwe trip, there were six of us who saw the black mamba, and it was a topic we discussed around the campfire that night. Only two of us had not lost a relative to that snake! Gray Watson, the principal of our Bible Institute, was one of them, and I was the other.

We continued our trip to Kalengwa that afternoon, and as we rounded another corner there, standing on the side of the plain was a red hartebeest. There were probably others around, but only this one was visible. We desperately needed meat back at the Bible Institute, so we quietly got out of the Jeep, circled to the far side of a huge ant-hill, and shot. That was the easy part. The two of us did not have the strength to lift this antelope into my car, but Fainoti had a plan. We tied one end of a thin cable on the back legs of the animal and the other end on to the hitch of my car. We dragged it until we straddled a one-meter-high anthill. I then reversed the Jeep and rolled it into my car!

About twenty kilometers on, we saw a second full-grown mamba straddling the road. This one did not rear as we drove over it. Two mambas in one day, but that was not the end of it. A young geologist came out to meet us as we drove into Kalengwa Mine.

"Roy," he said, "we caught a one-and-a-half-meter mamba earlier this morning, and we are planning on selling it to the snake park on the copper belt. Come and have a look." The snake was in a vegetable safe, used in the early days to keep flies and other bugs from contaminating food. They were feeding the mamba with white mice, and we got an immediate demonstration of the power of the poison.

The geologist had four or five books on snakes on the top of the safe in his office. There was only one I had not read, so I opened it to the chapter on mambas and read a firsthand account of two hunters in Zambia, one of whom was bitten by a black mamba. The details of his death and the actions of the mamba became key information for me exactly one week later

It was late November 1964. The rains had come, the grass was green, and wildflowers abounded in the bush. The previous year, we had completed an airstrip for the small four-seater Cessna based at the hospital at Mukinge. As we were expecting visitors to fly in the next day, I needed to inspect the airstrip; and Gwyn, who was eight months pregnant, asked me to pick a bunch of wildflowers on the way.

Two rivers met near our institute. The Kalende ran into the Kalambo, and about seven kilometers farther on, that ran into the mighty Kabompo River. The Ba Kaonde had isolated villages, and the Ba Chokwe had begun to multiply as they fled the upheavals of Angola in the northwest. The real originals were the snakes and wild animals that had abounded for thousands of years.

Growing up in Africa, I had developed what people called snake eyes. Living at Chizera caused me to hone those skills. As I neared the airstrip, I had an armful of flame lilies and an eagle eye on the undergrowth. But this snake came up from behind. I heard a sudden swish and then felt the sharp pain on my right calf. I leapt in the air, turning my head at the same time. The black mamba, really a gunmetal gray, was the snake I least wanted to see in these circumstances. I knew that I had a death sentence and very limited time left. Mambas inject a paralyzing neurotoxin. This one went off at a great pace with its head a half meter from the ground, and twenty meters away, it swung its body around with its head well above the ground and fixed its eyes on me.

One scene from the chapter on the two hunters I had read about earlier came back to me. I did not know whether to believe it when I read it, but I believed it now. After biting his friend, that mamba had also stopped twenty meters away. He was so busy attending to his friend, who, after twelve to fifteen minutes, had lost consciousness, that he only occasionally glanced in the direction of the snake. Suddenly it came again. In panic, he heaved his friend aside to attempt to get away. The mamba went for his friend again and bit him a second time. When I had read that, it seemed plain speculative theory, even exaggeration. I know the snake experts were not all agreed on this theory, but at that moment, I was not going to wait around to confirm it.

My normal experience over the years when I met a mamba, small or large, was it very quickly got out of my way. If you corner them or if they have a nest with eggs or newly hatched babies, they become aggressive. Now, a puff adder, night adder, or Gaboon viper are different. They are fat and sluggish, and if you step on or near them, you will get bitten, and with lightning speed, nothing sluggish about the strike.

Mambas are bewildered if they lose sight of you. I knew this, so I jumped behind a huge tree. I was carrying a handkerchief, so I bound it very tightly just below the knee so that it would form a tourniquet. Up to this date, there was no one in the history of Zambia who had survived the bite of a mamba, so I knew that I had little time to try and get home to say good-bye to my wife. I peeped around the tree. The mamba was still in place, and so keeping the tree between me and the snake, I walked away then hopped with speed the next two hundred meters back to our mission property. I was young, fast, and frightened.

Jonas Kibinda, one of the students, was slashing grass near our home, and I yelled to him in Kikaonde and told him to go and inform the Wrights that a black mamba had bitten me, and then to go and tell the students of my emergency. Ginger and Dulcie Wright had come over to the Bible Institute for a year while the principal, Gray Watson, and his wife, Mary, were on furlough. Ginger, an Oxford scholar, was a veteran translator and teacher. He spoke Kikaonde with an Oxford accent, but his grammar and accuracy qualified him to be one of our Bible translators. The people loved the Wrights, and we were privileged to have them with us for that year.

All of our mission stations in Zambia were linked up by radio, and we had three call-up times each day: 7:30 a.m., 10:30 a.m., and 5:15 p.m. I was bitten at approximately 5:13 p.m., so Ginger was able to go straight on the radio and interrupt everybody with the emergency call to our hospital at Mukinge and call for prayer from the whole network. Phone calls were made to all our home councils in Canada, USA, Britain, and South Africa; and within minutes, people around the world were calling on the Lord on my behalf.

The doctor and surgeon at Mukinge was Alex Henderson, a missionary from Canada with service in Angola and Zambia. It was too late for him to come by plane, so Alex packed all the necessary medication and equipment into the hospital station wagon. He knew that I knew snakes in the African context, so he also packed a body bag! He never expected to see me alive. Accompanied by our Zambian director Clare Gifford and by his wife, Blanche, they set off on a journey of 160 kilometers, which would normally take three hours; but with little conversation and lots of prayer, they sought to avoid the potholes and corrugations and broke all records.

Meanwhile, I just made it to our kitchen door when my legs were paralyzed, and I collapsed on the floor. Hearing the commotion, Gwyn, my very pregnant wife, a nurse who had already treated many snakebites, came rushing in. The only serum that she had was the regular tropical serum as the mamba serum was still being tested. That had never saved anyone from the poison of the black mamba.

Gwyn injected this serum around the bite and in the thigh and shoulder. She then lanced the bite and sucked it to try and draw out as much poison as possible. This is not practiced anymore but was standard procedure then. Being eight months pregnant with our daughter, Janice, the sixty-meter run to the clinic and the stressful anxiety of treating me where I had collapsed on the kitchen floor was no help in her condition, and now and again, her hand went to her abdomen. This made me think that maybe the baby would come early, and so my focus shifted from my needs to hers.

Our eldest son, Douglas, was nearly four years old, and a few days earlier, I had made him a cotton reel tractor, a simple and easy-to-make toy that had given him hours of delight. It started with an empty wooden cotton reel. By cutting grooves in the reels and thread-ing a rubber band through the hole with a small piece of candle threaded too, and then a with a big stick at one end and a smaller end at the other, the action of winding the smaller stick gave it traction, and it would go forward like a real tractor. Doug was distressed as the rubber band had broken, and a new piece of candle was required. Totally unaware of the crisis playing out in the life of his daddy, he knelt down and shook my shoulder.

"Daddy, Daddy, you promised to fix my cotton reel tractor."

Jewel Remboldt, one of our single missionaries, decided that both the boys needed to be out of the way and took them to her house. I heard his voice asking, "What about my tractor?" I won-dered if I would ever see these precious little lads again.

Meanwhile, our students had gathered and were kneeling in urgent prayer outside the kitchen. I was giving Gwyn a commentary of how the paralysis was creeping up my body. At a very critical junc-ture, one of our senior students, who eventually became one of our national staff, entered. Fainoti Kalubenyi had accompanied me on my trip to Kalengwa to get the tsetse-fly medication for our dog. He and I were very close. He asked in Kikaonde, "What snake bit you?" As soon as I said the word *nkonkola* (mamba), his color changed, and his eyes were wide, unblinking and full of fear.

I spoke what I believed at that moment, "I am going home to be with the Lord. You will stay here, and there is so much to be done for the Lord."

His eyes came down to the right size, and with his finger pointing down at me, he said, "You have been bitten by a black mamba, but we have a great God, and we are going to pray."

Lots of people were praying, but there was something special about the tone and authority of his prayer. I was challenged to believe that this situation could be turned around. The whole country seemed to scream, "That is not possible. We have the facts: you will die."

As Gwyn checked my pulse, she noticed that it was getting weaker, and she ran awkwardly down to the clinic again to find a heart stimulant, all the while desperately praying for a miracle and yet seeking to be accepting of the will of the Lord. Just after she got back, sure enough, she lost my pulse, and immediately she administered the heart stimulant and found the pulse again. I had lost consciousness, and Gwyn asked a few of the men to carry me through to our bedroom. If I had died from that paralyzing poison, it would have been a painless way to go.

I woke up at about 8:30 p.m. There was searing pain under my arms. Every nerve and gland seemed to be on fire. If only I had a knife, I thought I could ease the pressure and pain. The bed was wet with my perspiration as I thrashed about. The strongest medication Gwyn was allowed to carry in our bush clinic was codeine. I'm not sure how many I had taken, but they did not touch the pain.

A very worried-looking Dr. Alex Henderson walked into our room just after 9:00 p.m. He injected an ampoule of Pethidine, expecting immediate results. He said that in his entire medical career, he had never used more than two ampoules. After he injected the third ampoule, I lost consciousness.

Sometime after midnight, there was a knock at the door. Fainoti's wife had gone into labor. Would Gwyn please come quickly?

"Fainoti", she said, "I am also having labor pains. Our child may arrive tonight, and I also need to be here for my husband."

She gave him some medical supplies and asked him to seek help from one of the other wives. As it turned out, Gwyn went to his home after 8:00 a.m. and delivered their baby.

Pethidine was taking care of the pain. My vitals checked out. I had not got up to go to the toilet; otherwise, I would have discovered that I was paralyzed from the waist down. Only after the doctor had departed to go back to his busy hospital duties that I spoke about not being able to urinate. Gwyn panicked, but God was in control. Dr. Alex had no peace about his decision, and just a couple of kilometers down our bush road, they turned around to pick up our family of four and take us back to Mukinge Hospital. What a mercy!

Complications abounded. They decided to give me the tropical serum over again in an attempt to overcome the paralysis. I had a serum reaction and went into shock. My whole world spun out of control. I despaired of life. After another shot, I lost consciousness again.

Five days passed. Though the care was amazing, I remained paralyzed from the waist down. Dr. Alex came to the ward after supper, put in a new urinary catheter, and told me that hope of life coming back to my legs was fading and that I would be in a wheelchair for the rest of my life. A dark cloud hung over my head, and despair seemed to inch its way to every corner of my being. I lay alone in the darkness of that night and wished to die. A thought flashed into my mind. What about Mike Warburton? We were the closest of friends, and we loved to stop at Mutanda where we had done language and share fellowship. A civil engineer at six feet four, he had married one of our nursing sisters, Francis Wood. They had two children, Mickie and Tricia. Then spinal meningitis struck. In his book *From Where I Sit*, Mike tells the story of how God cut him in half and doubled his effectiveness. He had spent two years at Stoke Mandeville in the UK and learned how to operate from a wheelchair. In the early hours of that morning, Mike's story was an inspiration. I apologized to the Lord for my death wish and knew that, by the grace of God, I too could learn to operate out of a wheelchair.

What happened next still brings tears to my eyes. Lying there in the darkness of that long night of despair and victory, I suddenly felt an involuntary twitch in the muscles of my left calf. That, I thought, had to be life coming back. I found a pin from my bedside table and plunged it into my left leg. No pain; therefore, no life. The hopelessness returned. Moments later, another twitch. I was sure this time. I called out for the night sister on duty, Phyllis Spahr. Phyllis rolled up my pajama trouser legs, and we shared a comic moment. Paralysis had diminished much of the muscle and flesh. As she held up her kerosene lantern looking for the movement I had reported, I said, "Sexy legs, hey?" She laughed and then called out joyfully, "I saw the twitch. Your legs are coming back." I don't think the doctor was thrilled about being called at that unearthly hour of the morning, but he also saw the movement and explained the medical facts that were unfolding. We all rejoiced together. Intensive physiotherapy and learning how to walk again signaled an amazing victory in Zambian medical history as my life was not only spared, but I got the full use back in both legs.

News reached Chizera that we were coming home. Nothing humbles me more than the events that followed. The dusty road was lined with people from villages and our Bible school. They ran beside the car, ululating and leaping joyfully.

As I hobbled toward the back door of our house, a brown house snake slithered away. I involuntarily went into a cold sweat. I felt such shame, especially as the snake is nonpoisonous. As a boy, I had one as a pet. In the next week, no fewer than thirteen snakes visited us, including a muswema (a tropical mamba) and two spitting cobras. Normally, I would not have been counting, but that was not a normal time. It was as though that old snake, the devil, was not too pleased with the outcome.

In the days that followed, many told me of a family member who had died as a result of the bite of the black mamba. In fact, almost every student had lost a family member or extended family member to that snake. If I had not been bitten, I would never have asked questions like that.

I have always felt just a little jealous of the apostle Paul, who, on the island of Malta, while gathering some wood, was bitten on the hand by a poisonous viper, which he shook off into the fire; and to the amazement of the island people, who expected him to swell up and then die, he continued his ministry of healing and preaching. The purposes of God are worked out in a great variety of circumstances, and as we trace His unmistakable and merciful hand, we give Him all the glory.

On a ministry trip to Northern Ireland, Steve Stockwell, the chaplain to the University of Belfast, who had married the daughter of our Irish representatives, Bryan and Anne Gordon, came to hear me at the Bangor Conference Center. He put a couple of my stories together in this poem: the one on the snakebite and the freedom fighter I picked up at Chimanimani. Both stories take us to Calvary. Steve is a much-loved preacher and poet.

"Black Mamba Sleeps"
for Roy Comrie by Steve Stockwell

Black Mamba rages
With a killer bite
Poison tongued intentions
Spitting his spite
Lingering death amusement
Fun in ferocious fear
On the very edge of hell
You take him away from here
To the lies and the spit
The slaps and clenching fists
To the whips and scourging lashes
To the thorns and angry twists
The hammer crash on flesh and bone
The shrieks of fury and pain
The breather into suffocation
Then the harrowing agony again
You stand and meet his stare
Peer into his silence
Treat him with deep respect
Show him an even more violent violence
No one survives this merciless place
Yet you walk away somehow
Black Mamba looks up at you and smiles
"Baba Comrie I'm sleeping now

Steve took me to the University of Belfast at 9:30 p.m. one Sunday night. I was amazed how this insightful young chaplain—through questions, answers, and applications to a huge attentive student body—led us into a powerful meeting with God till the early hours. I learned deep and relevant applications to these stories, which incidentally are sixteen years apart!

Chapter 6

THE WITCHDOCTOR AT MUNYAMBALA

It would not be thought wise when the rainy season was at its height to start a new preaching point at Munyambala, a somewhat isolated village in Zambia. Moreover, the most powerful witch doctor in Chief Chizera's area lived there. Earlier efforts to begin a work there had failed, but one lonely Christian voice there was pleading for our help.

Three of our Bible school students needed a practical assignment, and it was my job to oversee their activities. So one Sunday morning, we set off, grateful that the rains had held off; and though the road was still a mass of mud puddles, I rejoiced in having a four-wheel drive vehicle, and we arrived in good time.

Soon after we had arrived and left our vehicle, unknown to us at the time, the witch doctor came to it. Our return to the car hours later triggered alarm and fear, especially in the eyes of our students. It was like a declaration of war. Ugly ingredients had been stuffed into cracks in the front, sides, and back of my car. He must have spent quite some time there with his magic and his medicine. The meaning became known as the students shared their alarm. We had been cursed by the most powerful witch doctor in our province. The fear of the witch doctor in Africa is huge. When something like this happens, it would stir up all kinds of thoughts and beliefs that we would suffer some catastrophe on the way home, or worse, there was even the possibility of death.

I can still remember the content of the prayer that followed: "Lord, we have no strength in and of ourselves to overcome the power of this curse, and so in the name of our Lord and Savior Jesus Christ, and on the basis of His death and resurrection, we come. Would You undo this curse, and as we journey home, would You protect us with the covering of Your blood shed on the cross." We journeyed home in safety.

During the next week, we learned more from two other friends on how to experience victory in this conflict of kingdoms. Neither had been with us on the previous trip, and as we were returning the next Sunday, we listened and learned from those who had dealt with such things in their past. One was a senior student, Fainoti Kalubenyi, and the other was a veteran missionary, Ginger Wright. He was an MA from Oxford who had worked among the Ba Kaonde for decades. Fainoti had worked with him in the Mutanda area, and together, they taught us lessons that we desperately needed to know.

The next Sunday, we were up early; and with a mixture of fear and faith, we set out once again for Munyambala. I parked in exactly the same spot, but instead of going into the school classroom, I circled slowly around the building and went back to my car. Sure enough, the witch doctor was already there and had begun his incantations. For the first time in my experience in Zambia, my greeting to him in his language was totally disregarded. I asked him what he was doing, and he replied, "You will see." I told him that I knew what he was doing.

"Last Sunday, you put a curse on my car and its occupants. When we saw what you had done, we knew how great was your power and the power of your curse. We knew that we personally had no power to overcome, so we prayed to our God, and when you have finished today, we will come back and pray that God will undo the stronger curse that you are using and allow us to travel safely to our homes." I added with emphasis, "We respect you and your power, but our God has all power, and we will pray to Him."

The worship seemed longer than ever, but finally we got back to my car. There was no sign of the witch doctor but plenty of evidence of his work. The prayers were fervent and believing, and we traveled home with a deep sense of the Lord's protection and power.

Many Sundays went by with no sign of the witch doctor. A growing number of the villagers turned in repentance and faith to the Lord and requested the help of a full-time man. Our evangelical church in Zambia assigned Evangelist Kyonaune and his wife and family to Munyambala. He was an experienced worker, and after only a few months of ministry there, he led the witch doctor to faith in Christ.

What followed was like a reenactment of the book of Acts. A huge fire was made just outside the witch doctor's house. I will never forget his joy in carrying all the paraphernalia of his craft and throwing those ugly pieces on the fire. Never will we forget the triumphant singing of the people and the conviction in the voice of the witch doctor as he gave testimony to his faith in a God whose power and love was greater than anything he had ever known. Never will we forget the humble, excited message of Evangelist Kyonaune as he gave all the glory back to our amazing Heavenly Father.

I was teaching a class in the vernacular one Friday morning at Chizera Bible Institute when there was a knock on the door. There was an urgent message for one of our students, Ba Beling Kyamulemba. His uncle had gone hunting, and contrary to their culture, he had gone alone. Only this time, three days had passed.

Ba Beling left the class and joined a search party that was getting ready to go. They knew where the uncle hunted and began to track his movements. The tracks led the search party to an area that they could only describe as confusing. It looked like there had been a huge scuffle, and the only tracks leading away were a very distinct zigzag on the ground.

They followed this to an area where the bush was so dense that they could only follow on their bellies. That was unnerving. Thirty or forty meters in, they came face-to-face with a five-meter python, with a full-grown man in his belly. It was fairly simple to kill that python and to release his uncle from his hideous grave. The reason for the distinct zigzag marks that were so evident on the ground, and which they followed, was because pythons kill their prey by knocking them down with the side of their head, and then with electrifying speed, they coil around their prey, and their constricting power breaks almost every bone in a man's body. What the python was unable to do, however, was to dislodge the small Kaonde ax from the belt of the uncle. The pointed end of the ax's head was pushing on the belly of the Python, resulting in a zigzag pattern as the python snaked its way into the undergrowth.

His funeral was unforgettable. Not because the uncle had any testimony but because his gruesome death attracted huge attendance, and Pastor Nenechi maximized the opportunity and pressed the claims of Christ to a very needy group of people. His graphic on Satan as a snake helped everyone present to see that it was only Christ who could overcome the awesome power of such an enemy.

We kept that python skin at Chizera, and when Bob Mosier visited us from Washington State, inevitably he heard the story. He had an insatiable appetite for snake stories. Not content to hear the story, he wanted to go to where the incident took place, so he had a total reenactment of my black-mamba saga, living out every moment of it. On the day that he arrived by plane, knowing of his interest, I had killed three snakes that morning; and rather than decapitate them and throw them into the bush as I usually did, I hung them over the washing line so that I could give Bob the background to each snake. He was enthralled as one was a tropical mamba with a neurotoxic bite, which affects the central nervous system. The other was a lazy, sluggish puff adder with a lightning bite and the most amazing camouflage. There are more fatalities from this snake than any other in Africa; It takes about twenty-six hours to die. Painful too. The last one was a twig snake, back-fanged, only slightly toxic. They are masters of deception, looking just like the roots among which they lie.

After lunch, we were going to fix the light plant engine, so Bob accepted the overalls we offered, saying that he was not afraid to get his hands dirty. We had only been working there a few minutes when our two-and-a-half-year-old son, Andrew, said, "Snake, snake." Sure enough, there was a nonpoisonous brown house snake trying to swallow a frog. Bob looked on from a distance. Just over an hour later, a student working nearby shouted out, "Mulolo" ("snake"). It was a small cobra.

A student working with us grabbed the twelve-foot hosepipe used for syphoning diesel. Bob put a bit of distance between himself and the snake. As the hosepipe came down on the snake, about fourteen inches of the aging pipe broke off, and would you believe it? The piece of pipe flew through the air toward Bob. There was a very high-pitched scream, and Bob took off for our house. He appeared meekly in time for supper, seemingly having lost all interest in the subject of snakes! To his credit, Bob went back to the States and applied to come back to Zambia as a missionary. He served with distinction for a number of years on the Copperbelt in our Christian Bookstore. Yeah, we had lots of fun out there!

Chapter 7

◆ • ◆

THE PREY OVERCOMES
THE PREDATOR

It was a Saturday afternoon, and Finoti and I were down at the wild Kabompo River for some fellowship and fishing. A massive crocodile scuttled noisily into the river as we arrived. We had not had time to dig for worms, so we both attached the big red Zambezi aristocrat lure and cast as far as we could, rewinding slowly.

Finoti had the first strike. It was a tiger fish and reputed to be one of the greatest fighting river fish in the world. Before he had managed to bring his catch to the river bank, I had a strike. When we laid the two fish side by side, they were exactly the same size, probably from the same hatching. On our old scales, they weighed out at about fifteen pounds each, around seven kilograms. This was an excellent beginning.

Before we could cast again, we saw it. Nothing could have interrupted our fishing except a giant African fish eagle. This legendary bird, with its haunting call and exemplary track record, caused us to lay down our rods. It was circling right over our stretch of the river. The speed and angle of its entrance into the water had us both entranced. If only I had a video. With its claws outstretched, it hit the water, and its talons went into the back of a massive tiger fish. We had both seen smaller fish extracted by this eagle, but this was extreme optimism, or was it greed?

What followed was riveting for us both. The closeness of it all made the sights and sounds all the more graphic and gripping. The eagle could not make an immediate getaway. Its massive wings beat the water, and slowly it rose with its prized tiger fish. As soon as it was clear of the water, the fish began its violent flapping, which caused the eagle to lose its balance; and from two meters above the water, it fell back into the river, still clutching its prey. The fish swam downward, pulling the eagle with it. Both Finoti and I were trying to give the eagle advice, "Let it go, let it go." Whether it wouldn't or couldn't, we did not know, but that was no ordinary eagle. It drove its wings, now wet, and once again lifted the fish clear of the water. But the violent flapping resumed once again, and it took the eagle off balance. This time, the tiger fish hit the water, swimming! It took the eagle deep down to its drowning. Both of us had a sense of sadness and loss to see such a majestic eagle suffer such an undignified death. It floated to the surface and then drifted toward the bend of the river. We saw it suddenly being dragged under, probably by a crocodile, no doubt grateful for a free and sumptuous meal.

Finoti was the first to speak. "That eagle," he said, "is just like us. Like him, we were meant to reign and soar and have dominion, but like him, we get greedy. Instead of letting go and living to soar again, he held on to his poor choice, and it cost him everything."

I have told this children's story on all five continents around our world. I always begin the story by asking the children whether there are any tigers in Africa? Hands go up, and the kids are right into the Kabompo River story. Scores have understood the application and have learned to let go of the things that entice but also destroy. I sometimes thought that the adults were paying just as much attention as the children. Nowadays, you hardly ever hear a children's story in a church service. They don't know what they are missing! It is more than a message to children; it's a message to parents and others that children are special.

The Witch Doctor Faces Justice

It was big news in our district. The new Zambia police had arrested one of our well-known witch doctors and charged him with a serious crime. The magistrate was at Chizera, and conviction seemed inevitable. The sentence was pronounced. The witch doctor was going to prison for three years.

As the accused was shuffling out in his leg-irons, he stopped at the desk of the clerk of the court. He did not blame the magistrate who had pronounced the sentence, but this clerk who had written it in a record book was the one he chose. Looking the clerk in the eyes, he said, "Tomorrow in the late afternoon, someone in your house is going to die." The clerk, an educated Zambian man, rejected the curse, saying he no longer believed in witchcraft.

The next afternoon, at around four o'clock, a massive storm came up. The thunder and lightning drew nearer until there was a mighty bang as both the thunder and the lightning struck together. At the height of the storm, one house in the Chizera-Boma area was struck by lightning, cutting it in two, and a woman and her two children inside were knocked unconscious. As the clerk of the court approached his home, he took one look inside and was struck with a paralyzing fear. Thinking that his whole family had been killed, he ran off into the bush and hid.

Around five o'clock the next morning, standing outside the door of my office at Chizera Bible Institute was one of the most frightened men I have ever seen. It was the clerk of the court. Through the night, he had come on foot to ask for help. He was beyond desperation, and the story he told was almost beyond belief. He knew that we had radio contact three times a day to our stations in Zambia, and he wanted a message sent through our Mukinge Hospital to the Boma at Kasempa to call the district secretary, the police, and even the army to come immediately and rescue him.

After I had listened to his story, I told him that I would send his message but that the call-up time was 7:30 a.m., and we still had just over two hours to wait. I told him I would take him home, and it was with great reluctance that he got into my vehicle.

When we got to his home, he refused to leave the car, so I went in alone. Sure enough, his home had been cut in two by a searing lightning strike. The door was open, but there was nobody home. I ran to the next house, and they told me that the wife and two children had been taken to the local clinic. We drove to the clinic, where he found his wife and two children sitting on the floor on mats. They had been treated for burns and were in shock, but nobody was dead.

After our experience with the witch doctor at Munyambara, we have learned to genuinely love and respect the witch doctors. None of them are beyond the reach of our all-powerful and forgiving God. Experience has taught us to differentiate between the horror and the power of their practice, and their weakness and need as human beings. We also learned that there are two main groupings of witch doctors in Zambia. Vanangas (witch doctors) are herbalists or medicine men who seek to cure through natural remedies. Vananga Valubuko are witch doctors who consult with spirit powers, toss bones, and can manifest a supernatural evil power. The one we were dealing with was in this category.

The clerk of the Chizera court waited just long enough for his wife and children to be released from the clinic. I never sent that message over the radio, nor was I able to get through to the clerk on the greater power and the mercy of our Sovereign God. Terrified, he and his family fled our district with an understandable paralyzing fear.

Satan is a spirit being of immense power and influence. He is the god of this world, a liar, and a deceiver. Human choice has resulted in sin. Sin has brought death. Death has passed upon all of us. Our dilemma was answered by our Creator's amazing love in His redemptive act in His Son, our Lord and our Savior, Jesus Christ. There are no unimportant people to God. Religion, with its list of dos and don'ts, is a curse. Relationship with its message of, "It is done, it is finished, it is accomplished," is now reverberating around the world. God's family is emerging from every single ethnic group in the world.

Chapter 8

❖ • ❖

FORGIVENESS TRIUMPHS OVER EVIL

Marie Lawton came to Zambia in the early 1960s. She came as a high school teacher and taught at Mukinge Girls Secondary School. During her first term of service, she learned the local Ki Kaonde language well and also proved herself as a high school teacher.

When she returned from her first furlough after her first term on the field, it was with a burden to reach out with literacy training to the village folk around Mukinge. To do that, she converted her truck so she could have the ability to take her vehicle into the bush and have a place to sleep, prepare her own food, and live out there with the people. This became a very effective and wonderful way of serving the Lord.

One night, when she was back from the villages in her home, which was right on top of Mukinge Hill, a notorious criminal from Congo broke into her house. He tied her up, gagged her, put her in a corner, and proceeded to load most of her furniture and all her valuables into her truck. When he had completed that, he loaded Marie as well. About 2:00 a.m., he very quietly released the brake, started the car on the engine, and quietly drove into the night. It was one of those nights where it was pitch-dark, where you could not even see your hand in front of your face. When he got about seventeen miles away, he stopped the car and dragged Marie into the bush. He raped her and then began to beat her until she was bleeding, broken, and unconscious. Then he left.

The danger in a situation like that is very real. There are predators like lion, leopard, hyenas, and snakes, especially the python that could easily have made a meal of Marie. When she came to, she could hardly see anything. She had no idea where she was or where the main road was, but because of her intimate and wonderful relationship with her Savior, she prayed, "Lord, you are my Shepherd. I have no idea which way to crawl to go to the road. Would you please guide me?"

Not surprisingly, she crawled straight to the road!

"Lord, thank you so much. You know that during the day, there are only a few cars that come on this road, and here we are at maybe three o'clock in the morning, and there's rarely a car on this road. But, Lord, you are Lord, and I desperately need transport. Would you please send that?"

Not a few minutes later, she heard the sound of an engine. Six men in a Land Rover were coming back from a party and were weaving their way home. You can imagine their shock when their headlights picked up a body, the shape of a woman, lying on the road. They stopped just in time and immediately recognized her.

"Ms. Lawton, what are you doing here?"

The whole experience seemed to sober them up.

"It doesn't matter," she said. "Please just get me back to the hospital, and then I'll tell you the story another time."

Dr. Alex Henderson was on duty that night at Mukinge Hospital, the same doctor who, just a few months earlier, had tended to my needs with my snakebite. He stitched Marie up, and he gave her all the very best possible medical treatment. Marie lay there in her hospital bed until the morning, and then she excused herself from the hospital and said, "I'll be back, but I do need to get a message out on the radio."

She went to the radio and spoke to those of us on duty on our radio network at 7:30 a.m. She broke into the whole procedure and told us of the events of that early morning and how she had been raped and beaten and then said, "I do not want you men out there to be angry. I have already forgiven the man who did this, and I would like you to pray with me that somehow, by the grace of God, he will be led to repentance and that God would reveal to him his purpose for his life."

Listening to her story, I remembered very clearly that this man had actually become quite a legend. The stories of his escapades abounded. Once, after having been captured and put in prison, he was taken down to the local river with an armed guard to have his bath. He undressed, soaked his whole body, soaped it, and dove into the river, and that was the last that the policemen saw of him! They sent for reinforcements and searched upstream and downstream, but they did not find him.

Meanwhile, he had gotten out of the river and had doubled back to the police station where he stole some clothes and, from his hiding place, watched more policemen go to the river to search for him. He then put sand into all the petrol tanks of the Land Rovers except one, the one he stole. When the police tried to follow him a little later, their cars refused to start! He was a very astute man, and when he got to the next town, he dumped the police car and stole another car, which he took back into the Congo.

When we heard Marie reporting that she had been raped and beaten, we really were not thinking a lot about forgiving him. We were thinking much more that it would be better for the whole country if he was captured and put in prison. But God had other plans!

The man drove Marie's car with all of her stuff in it past Solwezi. He had made his own private road across the border into Congo, but what he did not realize was that there was a terrible storm just ahead of him, and the rain had turned his makeshift road into a quagmire. Marie's car went right down to the axel with the weight of all of her stuff. Amazingly, the police found Marie's vehicle with all the stolen goods in it. Her car was eventually returned to her.

The story doesn't end there. After abandoning Marie's car, he stole another car and took it back into Congo. Apparently, he decided that he had better stop operating in the Kasempa and Solwezi areas, and so he moved up to the northwest area where we were located. He stole another car. This time, the police in Kabompo caught him, retrieved the car, and imprisoned him in a makeshift barbed-wire prison near Kabompo.

There was a missionary from the Christian Mission in Many Lands (CMML) who went in as a worker into that prison. He noticed this huge man from Congo who stayed as far away from the Christian meetings as he could get. This missionary had a good voice, which carried to all the other inmates. As the weeks went by, this Congolese man got nearer and nearer and became a part of that little group; and with the passage of time, he repented and made a commitment to follow Jesus Christ as his Savior and Lord. He realized that he now needed to be truthful about his lifestyle. You see, the police had only arrested him on the charge of stealing one vehicle. They had not connected with the police in the other part of the province. So when he confessed to them all the vehicles that he had stolen and to the rape and beating of Marie, they retried him and gave him an extended sentence.

We had a Bible Institute not too far away, and we ran a correspondence school with the Emmaus courses. The missionary who was going into the prison had always used those courses, so he got in touch with us. Jewel Remboldt, one of our missionaries at Chizera who was in charge of our Bible Correspondence School, began to send out lessons to this man. He had a number of years to spend there, and in all of that time, he took eleven ten-week courses. He was a good student, well-disciplined, and his Bible knowledge and his love for the Lord grew steadily. He became a very mature Christian.

When, after a number of years, the time came for his release, he said, "My people only know me as a criminal. God has had mercy upon me. He has redeemed my life, discipled me, and now he has called me, and I want to go back to Congo and to Zaire as a missionary. But first, I must go to Mukinge, to that woman that I raped and almost murdered, and I must ask for her forgiveness."

Did he actually get there? Was he able to meet with Marie? I know it was his intention. I have to confess that I never heard about it. If he did get to Mukinge, Marie would have told him that right from the very day that he had raped her, she had forgiven him.

All contact with him was lost, and that's why heaven is going to be such a wonderful place to catch up and to hear of the things that God did with that man as he went back to his country as a Congolese missionary. The man who had been such a curse, we believe, became such a blessing. As a result of even what we heard, the contact that we had with him and with Marie, God taught us so many different lessons about forgiveness and about His mercy.

Chapter 9

THE TWO SAMSONS

Neither of these men was remotely like the Samson of the Bible. Samson Yamupendi was born blind. A caring mission to the blind, who loved him, taught him to read and write in Braille and enabled him to complete his high school, brought him up. They also led him to faith and maturity in Christ. Academically, he was the best student at our Bible Institute; and though he was fluent in five African languages, he was able to complete his three-year course in English. His Braille-writing and note-taking were a wonder for us all to see. He would read us his essays, tests, exams, and reports; and we, as the teaching staff, were always obliged to give him the top mark. His wife was also born blind, but they had three sighted children (Gwyn delivered one at Chizera). It was an education to watch this family in operation. The closeness, interaction, control, and loving care were a challenge and a blessing to observe.

We were coming to the end of a lengthy course, which I was teaching, on the life of Christ when Samson approached me with a request. Could he sing a song he had written to the whole class? He said it would summarize the lesson of the previous day. His song was amazing. The content was incredible, and his deep baritone voice brought melody and miracle, captivating us all. Gray Watson, our principal, wrote out the music, and soon Ba Kaonde everywhere were singing this new dynamic song.

When we came to the end of that semester, while bidding the Yamupendis' farewell, I suggested to Samson that he go back through his notes and, if he felt led by God, to write any more music we would be delighted to hear. Two months later, he came back with sixteen inspired melodies filled with content and class. God gave him incredible words and a new melody for each new song. It wasn't long before these and many other songs written by nationals were being sung in every one of our churches throughout the country of Zambia and in choir conferences, led by Gwen Amborski (Foulkes), who had training in ethnomusicology.

It was much later that Samson reminded me that he disagreed with my use of the term *unlike the biblical Samson* in that he accomplished his greatest work as a blind man. I had forgotten that the Samson of the Bible had accomplished more as a blind man than he did when he had his sight.

Samson Sumaili was the other Samson. He was no academic, but with a lot of hard work, he got through all of his classes. His training focused on the pastorate, but he kept telling me his calling was to be a church planter, having proved himself as one at Chizera.

A common site in colonial Africa was to see a white boss standing by while the black workers do the work. As I explained earlier, staff and students worked side by side. On weekend assignments, we would accompany the students on bicycles to destinations that were up to sixty kilometers away. I rode with Samson several times in the course of a ten-week semester to a place called Kikonge. We would arrive on a Friday evening and meet around a fire, singing, testifying, and then preaching and sharing with all the folks who came. We took no food but ate the cornmeal that they provided for us twice a day. Sometimes it came with vegetables, and occasionally, we even had chicken cooked by the local villagers who had not yet made any commitment to follow the Lord.

I listened in amazement and thankfulness as Samson shared the things we had been teaching them in the classroom. Our loving Heavenly Father watered that seed by the power of his Spirit, and fruit in that tough area began to abound. When they complained of not enough shade when we met on Sundays because the numbers kept increasing, we helped erect a simple shelter with a grass roof. A young boy of about seven or eight had been sent by his mother and was willing to help us. In time, Samson had the joy of pointing this young fellow by the name of Paul to the Savior.

Years later, after we had left Zambia and were ministering in Zimbabwe, I was invited back to speak at the annual Zambian spiritual life conference and also the annual conference of the evangelical church of Zambia. Paul Mususu was driving us from Lusaka, the capital, to Chizera, where we had worked. As we neared Kikonge, Paul asked if we remembered where we had first met, reminding me that he was that little boy whom Samson had led to the Lord way back in the 1960s. Paul had become not only the leader of our churches but of all evangelical churches in the country. We stopped to see his aged mother and remembered with thankfulness to God the humble beginnings of this great man of God.

After graduating, Samson, who was so greatly used by God to plant churches in the Chizera area, moved on to undertake the planting of more than ten churches in the Northern Province. After one of those trips, coming back to his home on the Copperbelt, he was tragically killed when the truck he was in was involved in an accident. Once again, we are reminded "how precious in the sight of the Lord is the death of his saints" and how hard it is for us to understand why. Only eternity will reveal the depth and the richness of the work that he undertook. Samson left a wife and five children, whom God provided for in amazing ways as they grew up.

Chapter 10

LIFE AT CHIZERA BIBLE INSTITUTE

Chizera Bible Institute (CBI) was located in the middle of a tribal people called the Ba Kaonde people. Their language is pure and melodious, such a joy to hear and a privilege to speak. The Ba Kaonde are patient, hospitable, and kind, with a very strong background in witchcraft. The school was a busy place, and our programs were relentless. Students came to us from Zambia, Congo, Angola, Zimbabwe, and Malawi.

Our isolation in the middle of the North-Western province of Zambia put us in the tsetse-fly belt and four hundred kilometers from the nearest town on the Copperbelt. Because of the terrible condition of the road, we normally only went to town once a year. In the 121 year history of our mission in Africa, poisonous snakes other than the black mamba have bitten thirty-seven people. Nobody has died. But combine the powdery dust, the heat, and the impatience of man on the terrible roads, and there is a long list of fatalities. Prayer before, during, and after a journey became standard. Some near misses sharpened our prayer skills. We certainly learned huge respect for the large animals and reptiles of Africa, but danger lurked on every dusty road.

Our many courses taught at the school were in both the vernacular and in English. With only one national staff member and two of us missionary teachers, we often found ourselves just one day ahead of our students. The writing, the typing, the mimeographing, and the teaching led to late nights and very early mornings.

The afternoons were given to practical work around the school. The work followed the principle of not delegating work to others but being fully involved in all that had to be done, such as the digging and loading of sand, the making and collecting of bricks and wood. We all were involved in repairing our six-kilometer stretch of road. We were able, therefore, to overcome the old colonial image of the white man standing by while the black man did the menial tasks.

Our principal at Chizera Bible Institute, Gray Watson, did his bachelor's and master's degrees at Wheaton. I fully realize the privilege of working for seven years, cheek by jowl, with such a godly, gracious, fun-filled, gentle man. When I go through the Galatians passage on the fruit of the Spirit, not one of that fruit was missing in him. He was born in Angola of missionary parents (his dad, Percy, is mentioned in chapter 4). His beautiful wife, Mary, soon after his death, wrote a booklet titled *True Tales from the Angolan Bush.* I got this story firsthand from Gray and will précis what Mary has written. When Gray was just seventeen months old in 1930, he contracted amoebic dysentery, responsible for the deaths of a countless number of children in tropical areas around the world. His worried parents, looking at his sunken eyes and inability to keep down any food, did not think he could live another forty-eight hours. Their isolation, hundreds of miles from the nearest city or doctors, focused their distress. Then came what they called a genuine miracle.

In the distance, walking toward them were two white men with African porters. They had been walking for weeks. The odds seemed impossible. Could this be the answer to their imploring prayers? Could one be a doctor? No, they were German speculators on their way to South Africa with the goal of discovering gold. They decided to stop over in Angola with the intention of bagging a leopard and some other big game. But they had a huge stainless steel medicine chest, with the latest medicines and a medical textbook. In that chest was a recently developed medication called Yatrin, a German medical scientific breakthrough to treat amoebic dysentery. Can you trace the unmistakable hand of God? The injections of Yatrin saved Gray's life. I know why! He was commissioned by God to work in Zambia and, later in his life, as a hospital chaplain in Canada. It was my privilege to be the speaker at his funeral.

The story of those speculators ended rather sadly. They successfully hunted and shot a huge leopard. Against the advice of Percy Watson and the Angolan hunters who said that leopards often pretend to be dead, they refused to put another shot into the leopard for fear of ruining their trophy skin. As they advanced to claim their prize, the leopard struck, mauling one hunter from his forehead to his legs. The Angolan spears did their work. They fashioned a simple stretcher and hurried the hot and weary miles back to the mission. Percy's wife, Arminda, had a degree in home economics, not nursing, and penicillin was still over a decade from discovery. After loving round-the-clock care, unfortunately, infection won out, and the hunter died thousands of miles from his home in Germany. Mr. Watson conducted a simple but dignified funeral. The grave was covered with marigolds. The other hunter returned to his native Germany. Gray said that, years later, he wrote to his parents to say that the only reason he could think of for that entire journey was to deliver that Yatrin for that dying baby boy. To our loving Heavenly

Father, that was an adequate reason, and a whole life and ministry was preserved.

Our wives taught in the women's school at Chizera in literacy, Bible, and home economics. Mary Watson and Gwyn shared clinic duties. In addition to her clinic duties, Gwyn was also the midwife, delivering many babies in very challenging situations and at strange times, usually at night or early morning. Just the business of living and growing most of our own vegetables and fruit, as well as rearing our own chickens and hunting for our own meat, was time-consuming.

We maintained nine different engines on the property, which included generators for our electricity, pumps for our water supply, and of course, our car's and truck's engines. On top of that, there were a thousand and one other practical chores to attend to, like keeping the mpazhi (fire ants) from killing the chickens! Being in the middle of nowhere, we had to improvise. So we dug a shallow trench all the way round our chicken run and filled it with ash. The ants would not cross that trench until a branch fell down across it, and then they had their bridge, and we had a setback.

Then there was the problem of preventing the eagles and the hawks from making an easy meal of those same chickens. And how do you keep the egg-eating snakes from depleting our meager supply? The Zambian solution was ingenious. When we knew that the snake was visiting, we hard-boiled one of the eggs so that when the snake swallowed it, it did not melt like butter but maintained its original shape. The wire mesh that let him into the chicken run did not allow him any escape. When I came to collect the eggs, I also had to pronounce judgment on the snake!

Some problems were too big to solve, like the elephants coming through and taking all our corn and bananas and ruining our vegetable garden. We couldn't think of anything big enough to boil to keep them away!

Kabompo River Memories

The stresses of our 24-7 demanding yet fulfilling ministry found release in occasional visits to the wild yet beautiful Kabompo River. The arrival of Keith and Cindy Frew in 1965 was special. Our similar backgrounds fostered fellowship, and the work could be shared. We also shared some of the fun times. We made our own road to a special secluded part of the Kabompo River. It involved building a rough bridge over one of the tributaries of the Kabompo River. In the rainy season, the river overflowed its bank, but during the winter dry season, the river returns to its regular channels, and the whole area is covered by beautiful green grass. The many hippopotamus in the area, along with their enormous appetites, would crop this grass, each animal eating over five hundred pounds a night.

One evening at dusk, the elephants came to the opposite bank at the Kabompo River. To get a better view for us all, Keith decided to drive their big family Chevrolet van up to the river and then shine his lights on the herd. While trying to get the lights better positioned on the elephants, the front wheels of the vehicle went over the bank. The drop-off into the river was about three meters.

We did not give one more thought to the elephants as we rushed to the rescue. With adrenaline pumping, I carried a log that Keith and I had labored over carrying into the camp. If only I could get that behind one of the back wheels. Meanwhile Cindy and Gwyn were making a valiant effort to keep the van from toppling into the river. Keith had his foot so hard on the brake that his leg was trembling. I backed my four-wheel drive Land Rover near to his van and quickly joined the cars with a chain. I picked up the slack and then slowly drove forward. The chain broke. By now, the front wheels of Keith's van had turned at right angles to the bank. Grabbing a shovel and a hoe, I began to hack at the riverbank to try to make furrows for the front wheels of Keith's vehicle. With his van hovering near its balance point, we reconnected the two cars with what remained of the chain and mercifully pulled the van to safety.

On another occasion, not too long after this, Keith and Cindy were doing their Kikaonde language training at Mukinge Hill, 160 kilometers away. After completing one segment of their training, they had a couple of days off and so drove to Chizera to be with us. We all decided we should have a barbecue (braaivleis) beside the Kabompo River. We all piled into my car, including our three children—Douglas (four), Andrew (two), and Janice (seven months)—along with the Frew's baby girl, Renee, and we drove the six kilometers on the bush road that led to the river.

It was a Thursday. We never went to the river on a Thursday, it being a school day! But this was special. In fact, it was a God appointment, as we were soon to discover. There was much excitement as we arrived at our picnic spot, only to find we were not alone. A large luggage trailer stood in the clearing and a boat on the riverbank, but there was no car. Suddenly a man appeared. He looked like a ghost and was trembling.

Not five minutes before we got there, he had left his new Peugeot 404 in neutral with the engine running and the hand brake on. Somehow, while he was in the process of attaching a cable from the car to the boat, the Peugeot began to move. It barreled down the gradient and, fortunately, at the last second, swerved away from him and the boat, somersaulting into the river. It lay upside down in the bottom of the river, and even though the water was clear, the car was barely visible. Up till the time of the accident, everything had gone well. He had filleted and iced three large cool boxes with bream (tilapia) and with large tiger fish. He just had to pull his small boat up and tie it on top of his trailer and then make his way home. Then in a matter of seconds, it all went wrong, and now his car was upside down in the river, and his nearest town was four hundred kilometers away!

Although I had a four-wheel drive and a cable, it was hopelessly inadequate for the job, and I didn't even waste time trying to pull the man's car out. Time was of the essence, and our barbecue would have to wait. Telling the man to wait while we went for help, we all piled back into our car and raced home. We reckoned it would be in the middle of the night before we would get back to him. Dropping our families off back in Chizera, Keith and I drove to the Kalengwa Mine some fifty-four kilometers away. This was the richest open-cast copper mine in the world. I went there every week by motorcycle to teach a Bible leadership class and to help grow our church that had mushroomed when the mine opened. We were reaching out to hundreds of mine laborers.

I connected with a number of the men who were the geologists and workers in that mine management and told them the situation. They mobilized a rescue team with the needed vehicles and winches, and by two o'clock the next morning, they had extracted the Peugeot from the river. The vehicle trailer and the boat were safety towed back all the way to the Copperbelt.

It was not until about five months later that the man came back to our mission in his Peugeot 404, now restored. He was incredibly thankful, and he brought me a gift of a beautiful fishing reel. He mentioned the word *miracle* when he spoke of our arrival five minutes after his nightmare. I told him that we never go to the Kabompo River more than once a month and that was the first time we had ever been on a Thursday. The miracle that I explained to him was that our loving, merciful, amazing Heavenly Father got us to the exact right place at the right time! He wholeheartedly agreed.

Chapter 11

✦ • ✦

THEOLOGICAL
EDUCATION BY
EXTENSION

Administration has never been my gifting, so when I was appointed
as principal of the Chizera Bible Institute (CBI), it raised great fears
of inadequacy. At the time, we were having difficulty finding students. The people whom we thought should come and train for ministry at CBI were out there, but they were not applying to come
because of work or local church responsibilities.

Dr. Fred Holland of the Brethren in Christ and I were investi-
gating a new movement that was mushrooming in Central America
in Guatemala under the leadership of Dr. Ralph Winter. It was
called by the rather extravagant name of Theological Education
by Extension, TEE for short. The idea was to take the training to
where the people were. I presented a paper to the annual meeting in
Zambia of our 140 mission personnel. They gave the program their
enthusiastic endorsement.

We started with five centers and 89 students, and the movement
spread rapidly around our country. When we left Zambia in 1971 for
our new appointment in Zimbabwe, it was to implement that same
program in that country. Hugh and Mary Rough took over TEE in
Zambia, and under their capable leadership, they went up to 1,600

students in scores of centers. Many different countries in Africa also began to adopt the program.

The students weren't the only ones to benefit from this program. One of our missionary doctors, Dr. Jim Foulkes, really battled with learning the language of KiKaonde. After persuading him to teach one of the TEE classes every week, his grasp of the language improved rapidly. In his book *To Africa with Love*, he acknowledges how meaningful and helpful it was and how it impacted so many people.

The Quest for Unity

In 1969, I was one of the speakers at our annual evangelical church of Zambia leadership conference at Itimpi acres on the Copperbelt. The theme was unity. For years, we had been battling for unity between the mission and the church. We had been given a list of seventeen items of disagreement submitted by the church leadership and realized that we were severely lacking in our understanding of the cultural-background information and application. We had no problem apologizing for the things that we had done but had a problem sincerely apologizing for things that were done in 1917 by some of our early missionaries who were no longer around to defend themselves. Our Zambian-national fellow workers have always understood us better than we understood them. Through their patient, loving care, the penny finally dropped. When the seventeen items causing disunity were presented to us, we were more than ready to accept the total blame and ask for forgiveness.

In the Zambian culture, deeds done by those associated with you, even fifty or one hundred years before, are your fault and your responsibility. The Lord enabled us to deeply understand and sincerely accept their view and to repent for what had been done not only by us but by those before us. The result was almost beyond belief. Nobody thought of supper that day. Instead, worship, praise, and thanksgiving abounded in our meeting until suddenly one national leader stood up and said, "We have given you our list. Do you have a list?" There was a brief moment of silence, and yes, we had written down a few things. Without hesitation, they asked for our forgiveness. It seemed as though there was no part that was dark. The air cleared, and the presence of the Lord was overwhelming. Grace was abounding. Time seemed irrelevant. Food and sleep had no meaning. Preeminently our enjoyment was of the Lord. Then imperceptibly yet daringly and deeply, we began to pray for one another and to worship our sovereign majestic Lord.

The business of the meeting for those few days was prayer, and in that context, we dealt with the proposal that I made on leadership training where I recommended we move into the Theological Education by Extension program. As soon as the biblical basis was understood, the program was accepted in principle, and a small working committee was formed, which would ensure its implementation depending on the outcome of the pilot scheme, which was already in operation in the Chizera district. This was never meant to replace the resident Bible colleges and seminaries but wonderfully dovetailed them, revealing hundreds of leaders who later pursued further training.

I doubt whether you would ever be able to find a minute from any of our meetings on the acceptance of the program called New Life for All. God was working mightily in Nigeria and in other countries in Central and South America, and now it was His time for Zambia. It came in by acclamation. Some people called it consensus. The truth is that unity will never, ever be created. The unity of the spirit can be kept only when we are born from above, like having that Nicodemus experience in John 3. Only when we walk in the spirit (Galatians 5:25), when we grow his fruit (Galatians 5:22), when we exercise his gifting (1 Corinthians 14:12), and when daily we receive his fullness (Ephesians 5:18) can we be assured of unity.

Anyone can split a church, but without love, patience, and mercy, we are nothing, and we gain nothing (1 Corinthians 13). As missionary statesman David Evans says in his book *Daily Encouragement*, "There is the danger of confusion as some desire the greater gifts without discerning which they are. Is there a way to ensure harmony and balance? Is there a way to keep the unity to glorify the Lord?

There is. The most excellent way. It is essential, without it, tongues, prophecy, mountain moving faith, martyrdom amount to noise and nothing."

It took me another twenty years to get perspective on this 1969 conference that we had at Itimpi acres in Zambia. In a studies program I did later, I wrote a paper on church growth and chose Zambia as the model. As I followed the graphs and statistics, I realized that prior to 1969, growth had been minimal. But the gradient was steep after 1969. The basic ingredient for this growth spurt was the discovery and experience of the unity of the spirit that God granted to us. In all our Christian history, there is so much blessing that tumbles in when we have that one heart, that singleness of vision. The greatest missionary text is John 13:35, where it says, "By this all men will know that you are my disciples, if you love one another." It's no wonder the enemy attacks us at this point of oneness and causes us to sling mud at one another and to become proud of our own abilities, which had come as gifts from our loving, caring Heavenly Father.

Chapter 12

* •

FLOODING IN ZAMBIA

The year 1969 was also the year the rains came. Our rivers filled and then overflowed. The roads became rivers, and stories of hardship and danger abounded. Whole villages were moving to higher ground. In one incident, a man was attacked on the main road by a crocodile, and he used his bicycle as a shield to fend off the aggression of the hungry reptile. People were catching fish on the main road, and only four-wheel-drive vehicles were risking any journey.

We had planned a trip to the Copperbelt with three of our senior students for three weeks of ministry to advertise our institute and challenge local churches on the Copperbelt. Road reports varied, but at the last minute, we got a green light. We had four hundred kilometers of terrifying flooded roads to go before we could reach the Copperbelt, and because of the extremity of the situation, we allowed two days for the journey. Richard Soko, Leonard Gondwe, and Martin Mavuya were outstanding students and gifted communicators. Lots of prayer had gone into this trip, and although the road and the program ahead were daunting, we were excited and reveled in the prospect of serving together.

The first two hundred kilometers was uneventful. It was only when we approached an area called Mujimanzovu, a low-lying plain area, that I changed to the low four-wheel-drive range. As we ground our way through the mud and water, the water level rose, and the road worsened. Huge trucks had lost the road and ended up almost completely submerged. Their cargo of maize meal, flour, and sugar had spilled into the water and rotted. The smell was nauseating. The drivers had abandoned their trucks and were nowhere to be seen. There was no village in sight.

In this muddy, flooded wilderness, the road seemed to suddenly drop away. The water soon covered the engine, and the putrid water began to flow through the windows of the Land Rover. Before long, the engine died. The car tilted dangerously, and I thought for sure that my valued Land Rover was history. We scrambled out of the windows on the right side, and although not one of the students could swim, we all made it safely to the higher ground on the side of the road. Apart from occasional mounds, this was all underwater, and with difficulty, we were all able to make our way down the road. I looked back at my car and wondered whether I would ever even see it again. Richard Soko was so nauseated that he lost the contents of his stomach.

About one-and-a-half kilometers down the road and just after 5:00 p.m., we came on a makeshift government road camp. But before we presented ourselves, we took a bath, fully clothed, in a ditch that had relatively clean water. There were four men along with their families in this tiny camp along with one huge D7 grader. They all spoke our Kaonde language, and after greeting them, I asked if they could help me rescue my Land Rover with the D7. I was told that I would have to wait until the next day as it was after 5:00 p.m., and nobody would pay them overtime. I asked him how much it would cost for the overtime, and he said it would be two kwacha, which would be no more than a dollar. Even I could afford that! The money was paid over, and as the darkness was descending, we jumped on the D7 and headed down the road toward my car.

When we got to the Land Rover, it was all but underwater, which meant one of us had to get wet to attach the tow chain! I looked inquisitively at our three students but knew it was going to be me. After all, it was my car, and it was leaning even farther to the right. It took half a dozen dives before I secured the chain. I swam through the driver's-side window and opened the back door of the

Land Rover to allow the massive buildup of mud and water a way out. I just got back into my seat when the D7 driver took off.

Darkness was falling as we arrived back at the camp. We had another bath in the ditch; a quick check under my car confirmed that the entire exhaust system had been torn away. At least I could not see any oil leak.

The road-camp workers were delighted that we were all fluent in their language. Their kindness and hospitality came in the form of two of the wives of these men. When they heard our story, they took our filthy, smelly sleeping bags and a lot of other things and washed them. They enlarged the fire outside and hung the bags nearby to begin the drying process. There was no way that we could use them that night, but the night was warm, and we stoked the fire and slept on the mats they provided.

While the night was still fairly young, they brought two pots of food, one filled with nshima, which is cornmeal, their staple food, and the other with the muriwo, which is the relish, cabbage and spinach.

Africans are born storytellers. Their history, culture, and humor are gripping. They laugh loudest and longest at the idiosyncrasies and shortcomings of the white man. Some years after David Livingstone found what has been called the first wonder of the world, Victoria Falls, Africans called it the "smoke that thunders" or *mosi-o-tunya*. Soon after, white hunters began to penetrate deep into the Zambian bush where hippopotamus abounded.

The local Africans found a novel way to make the white man share his bounty. They would make him crawl on his belly to the edge of the river where they would choose a big hippopotamus and indicate on their own bodies where the bullet was to go, just behind the ear. There were so many hippos that it was hard to count them, and as the shot rang out, the river would just seem to absorb all of the hippo, including the dead one, and everything went mysteriously quiet.

Knowing that the white hunter would not see the hippo he had shot, the Africans would suggest to the hunter that he may have missed and that they had seen a splash on the other side of the hippo where the bullet hit the water. But to suggest that he had missed from such close range was humiliating for the proud hunter. They knew that the hippo was dead and that his three tons of weight would keep him on the riverbed for eighty to ninety minutes until the gases had built up, and then he would float to the surface.

They also knew the impatience of the white man, so after about ten to fifteen minutes of waiting, they would assure the white hunter that there were many more hippos upstream. So off they would go to find another hippo. The villagers would then come and wait for the dead hippo to surface, and using a dugout canoe, they would tie a rope to the back of the hippo's legs and pull him to the bank. The men from the village would come and roll him onto the bank where everyone would be involved in the massive and joyous task of cutting up the animal. The meat would then be dried, and it would provide sustenance for months to come.

This process would be repeated three to four times until each of the villages in that area had an adequate supply of meat. Eventually, the white hunter would be taken to a shallower part of the river, where there were hippos lying or standing on a sandbank. There, the hunter would shoot the hippo and, this time, actually see it topple over on the bank, large as life but dead. All the hunter wanted was the fifteen to eighteen pounds of ivory in the hippo's teeth and a few pounds of tenderloin. Everybody was satisfied.

When we had all finished laughing, the storyteller asked me, the only white man there, "When that hunter got back to his homeland, how would he tell that same story to his friends?" They already knew, but they laughed uncontrollably when I confirmed the hunter's probable selectivity of facts in protecting his prowess as a hunter.

That night, Martin Mavuya shared his testimony, and God did an eternal work of grace, especially in the hearts of one of the families of those men who had helped us pull my car to safety. Not one of God's words will ever return to Him void, and we have many surprises waiting for us in heaven, when we see all the fruit of the work that was done along the way.

Every year, we shot one hippopotamus and three buffalos. This provided all the meat for one year for our students and their wives and families.

When there are good stories around the fire, Africans go to bed very late. This does not affect the time when they get up, usually well before dawn. We were up early as well, and leaving the fire where we had slept, we met around my car for prayer. We needed wisdom, mercy, and patience, and most of the morning was spent cleaning and drying out our effects. Two of us worked on the car, and the other two on the luggage and literature. We took apart all the electrics using borrowed rags to clean the distributor, the points, and the plugs. Amazingly, the fuel line was intact. After putting it all together again, we had another prayer meeting: "Please, Lord, let it start!" The engine hesitantly turned over, gave a few deathly coughs, and then sprang to life. It sounded like a drag racer, only louder.

We had said our good-byes to the men earlier, and now the women and a few children came. We thanked them profusely for their kindness and hospitality, and they thanked us for bringing the Word of God and for leaving them with Kaonde Bibles and hymnbooks and other literature. They said that the mud marks on the literature would always remind them of our visit.

Mutanda was our next stop, where Mike and Fran Warburton served. They barely recognized us, and when we saw ourselves in the bathroom mirror, we knew why. The garden hose followed by a shower completed our transformation. Mike, a civil engineer by profession, tells in his book *From Where I Sit* how the Lord cut him in half from six feet four to three feet two and doubled his effectiveness. After his marriage to Fran and his call into missionary service, Mike had suffered the devastation of spinal meningitis; and although he was restricted to a wheelchair, he proved repeatedly the biblical truth that when we are weak and admit it, that's when we can prove God's amazing power.

The three weeks of ministry on the Copperbelt took us to Chililabombwe, Chingola, Kitwe, Mufulira, and Ndola. The Lord did wonderful things in our hearts, and fruit abounded in every meeting. Many surrendered their lives to the Lord and committed to coming to Chizera Bible Institute to study. One day, we will be able to see all the fruit of that particular ministry trip. It cost a fortune for me to get my car fixed. Once again, we proved the principle of His provision. And now, after fifty-four years of service for Him, we have never, ever had any debt, and we give Him all the glory.

The Return Journey

We got safely back to Mutanda but now had to make our way back through the area where we had nearly buried my car on the way up. The rains had eased off, and there was just a possibility that we could get through. But I had first to make sure. Borrowing a bicycle, I rode the thirty-six kilometers to the road camp where we had spent an anxious night. I arrived just in time to see them hitch up a police Land Rover to the D7. Not wanting to take the chance of getting stuck like so many others had, including us, they had asked the road crew to tow them through the bad section. The Land Rover was brand-new, and the two policemen were immaculately dressed in their uniforms. In the cage at the back of the vehicle was an accused murderer.

Slowly, the D7 dragged them mercilessly down the road and into the mud and the mire. I kept pace with them, slopping my way through on the side of the road. If they got through this really bad stretch of road without damage to their car, I would risk it. It was a sad story and a very sorry sight. Almost at the exact spot that I had gone down, the putrid muck began to come through the windows of their Land Rover as the D7 relentlessly pulled them through. Had it not been a tragedy, it would have been hilariously funny. The police officers looked like they had been pulled through a pigpen, and the murderer in the back looked like he had been tried and found guilty. I was concerned for them, but my focus was on their car. Not only did they lose their entire exhaust system, but the sump had been smashed, and all the oil leaked out. I left them sending emergency radio messages to their headquarters in Kasempa.

After another fond farewell to the road-camp folk, I cycled back to Mutanda. I was certainly not going to navigate that road in its present condition. I would have to leave my car at Mutanda and find another way to get home.

I decided to call Gordie Bakkie at our Mukinge station to come and get us in the small mission plane and fly us back to Chizera. It all seemed so simple, but little did we know what lay ahead. Worse still, none of our students had ever flown.

After hours of bumping around on rotten, treacherous roads in my four-wheel drive, flying was exhilarating and smooth as silk. The students began to laugh and then sing, and as one later put it, "Why should I go around like a tick on the back of a donkey when I can soar like an eagle in a plane like this?"

About thirty kilometers out from Chizera, we saw them—black storm clouds from one horizon to the other straight ahead of us. The singing at the back of the plane stopped. I bravely suggested to Gordie that we go back to Mutanda or to Mukinge.

"No," he said, pointing to what looked like the eye of the storm. "We are committed. Chizera is only minutes away." It was also the only place he could refuel the plane for the return trip. We turned north, flying parallel to the storm, and looked for an opening to fly through. Suddenly he banked and went straight into the dark clouds. I would love to be a fly on the wall and listen in to what our students are telling their grandchildren about this adventure. From the silky smoothness at the beginning of our trip, we were now frighteningly being tossed around like a leaf. Gordie exhibited extraordinary flying ability. Death seemed very, very close at hand. After what seemed like forever, we broke through the clouds and flew just above the tall trees. We were filled with renewed hope as the little airstrip we had built at Chizera came into view.

We were on the final approach when Gordie pulled back on the stick. "We can't land here," he said. "The whole airstrip is underwater."

Almost immediately, I knew what we should do. There was a narrow straight piece of road that was on an incline that I was familiar with on my many trips to take TEE classes about twenty kilometers away.

But first, we had to get our intention across to Keith and Cynthia Frew on the ground so they could meet us on the road. Flying low over their house with the window of the plane open, we pointed and shouted, and somehow Keith caught on and got into his car and followed us. We circled a few times to make sure he did not miss the turnoff to Kalengwa. From the sky, our proposed airstrip looked like the narrowest of threads, but joy of all joys, it was wet but not flooded, and Gordie's landing was perfect.

We were cheering when the right wing hit a pole that a builder had propped up on the side of a culvert. The damage, however, was minimal; and we all climbed out, our feet once again on firm ground. By now, the storm had passed. I went over to Leonard Gondwe, one of the students. "Well, Leonard," I asked, "what did you think of your first flight?"

His eyes were wide and unblinking. "As for me," he said, "I was confessing all my sins."

We laughed, but it is amazing how much business one does with the Lord in moments like that.

When Keith arrived, we pushed the plane off the road, and Martin Mavuya agreed to stay with it while we went to get the aviation fuel. Would you believe it? We just crossed the little Kalende River bridge, just a kilometer from our institute, when Keith's car ran out of gas. With much laughter and joy, we pushed it home.

Chapter 13

OUR YEARS IN ZIMBABWE

It should have been all joy to go serve in the place of my birth. As a boy, I had learned the language of the Ndebele in a place called Balla Balla. There was not one other white boy there. All my friends were black. I was homeschooled by my mother, and because of the heat, classes started at 6:00 a.m. and were finished by 10:00 or 11:00 a.m. My friends were waiting and barefoot; we hunted, fished, and rode donkeys and young bulls that were just getting their horns. We knew the location of every wild fruit tree and the day the fruit would be ripe. They taught me how to make a catapult and how to use it for getting food. I learned different ways of trapping birds and small animals. My best friend Thabani took me to their home. His mother became like a second mother to me. I called her mother and never let on to my own birth mother. The recipe for language was relationship, and I dearly loved those friends.

Africans have a proverb in Ki Kaonde that says, "Matwi abiji, lujimi lunga? Lumotu" (two ears, one tongue). They said, "God gave us two ears and one tongue. We need to listen twice as much as we speak. Your ears will tell you when to speak. If you speak before you have listened, you will destroy the language." It works! I have proven it in learning my first language as a missionary in Zambia and did well enough to be asked to give a seminar on how to learn a foreign language. After reaching fluency in Zambia, it was expected that I would have no problem with the language in Zimbabwe. I fell hope-lessly short!

Our posting to Mutare was among the Ba Manyika people. In our churches, our members were all Ba Ndau. I requested permission for our family to spend three months at Rusitu to learn ChiNdau. I was told that they would only give us six weeks to go to Harare to learn Shona on the ninth floor of Livingstone House. With twen-ty-one noun classes and sixteen dialects, it was confusing. We mas-tered the grammar and ended up with 97 percent in the final exam-ination. We knew that we had not given adequate time to listening. Back in Mutare, they could understand us; but as ChiNdau is less than 40 percent Shona, we could not understand them. Over time, I sweated it out and eventually was able to preach and converse, but we never got anywhere near the fluency we had in Zambia. That was deeply disappointing to me.

Zimbabwe was complicated in more than just language. African nations had been galloping to independence in the 1950s and '60s, but the whites dug in their heels in Angola, Mozambique, Southern Rhodesia, South Africa, and South West Africa. When negotiations failed, war became inevitable. We lived through and ministered mainly to national peoples through those conflicts. This is not an opinion or explanation, just stories of what we saw God doing in the midst of these emergencies.

We lived in Mutare, a city on the eastern border of Zimbabwe. We could see into Mozambique, and we became a front line during the seven-year war. Forty-two missionaries were massacred, and over two hundred national pastors lost their lives. We were told that we were irresponsible bringing four children into such danger. Actually, we thought of danger differently. During our ten years in Zambia, malaria, sleeping sickness, hepatitis, and infectious and parasitic dis-eases surrounded us. With three rivers, we had the largest and most lethal snake population in the country, and predators abounded. We could never say, "If it is safe, we will stay or go." Zimbabwe looked like civilization to us, and it took a couple of years before the bombs began to fall. As the situation deteriorated, we saw the hand of God moving in mercy to every segment of the population. He was shaking our world and graphically revealing those things that are unshakeable.

In 1973, it was not the war clouds but a tragic accident that darkened our horizon. Steve and Delores Staurseth were longtime teachers at our Biriiri Secondary School. Three of their four children—Mike (fifteen), Ruth (thirteen), and Timothy (seven)—were boarding in our mission hostel in Salisbury (Harare). School was over, and arrangements were made for an ex-teacher from Biriiri, Betty Shephard, who had married Gerald Dallimore from England, to pick up the three children and bring them on the three-hour journey to our house in Mutare, where they would meet the Dallimores and travel together to Biriiri. Tragically, their new Citroën was involved in a head-on collision with a bus shortly after leaving Marandellas (Marondera). Betty was killed instantly. Ruth, their beautiful thirteen-year-old daughter, died on the way to the hospital. Timothy was in a coma, and he and Mike were taken to the hospital in Salisbury (Harare).

I got the phone call and was given the responsibility of passing on these tragic details to Steve and Delores when they arrived. Gwyn and I wept and prayed, dreading the sound of their car in our driveway. We pled for wisdom and compassion for us and courage for them. We were to be witnesses of the immediacy of the Lord's presence. Though we were told they had not been able to reach the parents, the police in Marondera did eventually get through, but they only said there had been an accident. Their fellow missionaries at Biriiri had taken up an offering to enable them to make the trip.

Before I said a word, Delores asked, "Which one of our children has died?" We shared what we knew and prayed together. From that moment, it seemed as though Steve and Delores were completely enfolded in our Shepherd's care. They sat clinging to each other in the back of their car as I drove them the long journey back to Salisbury. This beautiful couple sang worship songs in perfect harmony most of the way till we reached the scene of the accident. There was a lot of tangled metal, and I wanted to drive on by, but they insisted on stopping. The bus and car had been dragged off the road, but there were deep gouges on the road. We stood holding hands and prayed.

Angels had been there, and we were on holy ground. In Marandellas (Marondera) police station, I was able to identify the body of Ruth.

We were nearing Salisbury with a long line of cars coming toward us when suddenly a fast car came into our lane. With no place to merge, he missed us by a fraction, went off the road into the bush, through a ditch, knocked over a series of young trees, and came back through the ditch onto the road and sped off toward Mutare. We pulled off the road, stopped, and had another time of prayer. It was like a graphic from God to say, "You could all be dead. Your times are in My hands, and so are those of your children."

The parents saw their son Timothy in the Salisbury hospital, unconscious but still living. A little later, the parents gave permission for life supports to be removed as there were no brain waves. Mike did survive, though he was unconscious for six weeks and had brain surgery that removed the brain chips in his forehead, and he had to learn everything over again. He was left with a judgment and memory handicap.

Later, Steve and Delores told me they had no peace until they understood and accepted that what had happened was not God's permissive will but His perfect will. God entrusted them with the unthinkable. Their witness at the funeral in music and message was God-inspired, and the subsequent difficult years are filled with testimony to the faithfulness of theirs and our loving, caring Shepherd.

Chapter 14

CONFERENCES IN ENGLAND AND SCOTLAND

The Yom Kippur war had just started on October 6, 1973, when I arrived at Heathrow to speak at a number of conferences in England and Scotland. The whole airport inside and out was overflowing with Jews from around the world, all heading for Israel. It was a repeat of a previous visit to Heathrow airport when the six-day war had begun in 1967. I got there on June 8, and Jews from all over the world were heading for Israel. They came back to their land, but they have not yet come back to their Lord. When they do, Romans 11:23 will be fulfilled: "God is able to graft them back into the vine again." That will be a major event of history.

As I landed in Britain for the conference ministry, the cold air brought me first the sniffles then a bone-shaking influenza. As we began our journey to various centers in England and Scotland, I totally lost my appetite and got through the demanding programs by taking Anadin four times a day. After two weeks of ministry, I got over the flu and felt well enough to take the place of another conference speaker who had taken ill with the flu. But again, my flu rebounded, and I was back on Anadin and not eating properly. I flew out of Britain after a month of Anadin, but had good memories of folk in the conferences who had taken steps toward serving in a full-time capacity or with promises to pray or give.

Mike and Ruth Brandon met me at Toronto Pearson International Airport. I was to stay with them until Gwyn joined me. It was a cold, sunny day, and I tried to join in the fun and games with their children but felt nauseous. I blamed it on jet lag and went to bed early. In the middle of the night, I wanted to be sick and headed for the bathroom. Mike, thinking it was one of their children, came in behind me just as I blacked out. He caught me as I fell backward. When I came around, my concerned host, not getting any adequate replies, helped me to his car and drove me to the nearby Peel Memorial Hospital.

Knowing my date of arrival in Canada, our mission had made sure I was covered with medical insurance. Dr. Eric Braaten, a Christian, was on duty in emergency and quickly established that I was bleeding internally. I had a duodenal ulcer and ended up in the intensive care unit for three days, hovering between life and death. I learned that Anadin on an empty stomach for almost a month was extremely dangerous. Never have I felt so utterly weak. I apologized for my foolishness and asked the Lord to allow me to prove His promise that "His strength is made perfect in our weakness." After four days, Gwyn got word: "Roy is now out of danger." The problem was that she didn't know anything that had been going on. There had been a breakdown in communications.

I got a fright when I woke up on the fifth day to find that I was in a ward with three other men. One of them, Bob Hooper, was peering intently at me when I opened my eyes. "You're a Christian, aren't you?" he said. I thought maybe he had seen my Bible, but the bedside table was empty.

"Yes, I am," I replied weakly.

There was a long silence, and then he said, "How can I become a Christian?"

I was still receiving blood and oxygen and was in no state to give a coherent reply, but I was excited to be on duty for the Lord again. Bob was an alcoholic, in hospital for the sixth time to be dried out. His wife had left him, and his nine children had found refuge with their mother. He was like a desperate drowning man, and though I had grown up with an alcoholic father, I was silently crying out to the Lord for His wisdom and exactly the right words.

Directly opposite me was a very sick man who had just had open-heart surgery. Alec Robinson was a trucker. Obscenities flowed from his mouth except when his wife was present. I quickly understood that he would not put up with any "religious talk." As I took Bob down the Calvary road, I spoke so that Alec would hear every word. I was expecting some remark from him, but it never came. On one occasion, while Bob and I chatted for at least forty minutes, I noticed that Alec was reading a newspaper but never once turned a page. He was listening intently to Bob's prayer of repentance and faith. He knew the bondage that alcoholism had brought to Bob and never once mocked him as he began to express his thankfulness and joy in a relationship with Jesus Christ.

When I was sure of Bob's commitment, I asked after his wife. He told me that she was a long-suffering lady who had put up with his nonsense for years and would not be receptive to the story of his conversion. I decided to phone her and asked her if she could come to the hospital and meet me. Amazingly, she came and listened patiently to the story of her husband's conversion. After some questions, she agreed for me to bring Bob to the room and meet her. It was slowgoing, but it soon became evident that reconciliation was taking place, and she committed her life to Christ. Realizing that I was going back to Africa, I brought in a local pastor, Stuart Sylvester, who was able to integrate them into his church until a job opportunity took them to another Ontario town.

One day, a man nicknamed Giant, a fellow truck driver with Alec Robinson, came to visit him. Alec's wife told him that I was a believer. Giant came across to my bed. "Are you a Christian?" he boomed. If I hadn't been, I would have felt an urgency to quickly repent! He, Bob, and I met to pray for Alec, who had been resisting Christ for years. What happened next can only be understood in retrospect. Alec had another massive heart attack and was rushed up to the ICU where his life hung in the balance. The next day, when Dr. Braaten came to visit me, I asked whether I could go and visit Alec. "No," he said. "Only relatives are allowed in."

"I'm a pastor," I said, and permission was given. I went in my robe (dressing gown). Giant and Bob had prayed with me before this. I had learned from personal experience that the ICU is an intimidating place. Alec had tubes going in and out of him and was on oxygen. He could not speak, but he could hear. I held his hand and said, "Yes is two squeezes. No is one." I tested it out; he got it right.

"You have seen and heard what happened to Bob?" Two squeezes, yes. "You were listening to every word that I said to Bob." "Yes." I tested out to see whether he could say no. One squeeze. We were on track. "Would you like to ask for God's forgiveness and repent like Bob?" Two squeezes. I told him that I was going to pray. If he agreed, he knew how to say no or yes. I have rarely had a clearer indication of decision for God. He squeezed with more strength than I thought he possessed.

Alec's wife came to see me the next day. "What have you done with my husband?" Alarmed, I asked after him. "No," she said, "he is a changed man."

"How do you know?" I said.

"I have lived with him for years. Even if he could swear he wouldn't, he has changed completely."

I was coming to the end of my hospital stay when Alec's wife came in with a request from her husband, who knew he was dying. He wanted me to take his funeral. I agreed, and shortly after, I officiated at his funeral in one of the biggest funeral parlors in Brampton, Ontario. Truckers with their huge rigs arrived from all over North America, creating a major parking problem. The funeral home was filled to overflowing with people standing and looking in every window and doorway. I'm sure if the fire department had been there, we would have been closed down.

My privilege was to speak to that huge gathering and tell them the simple facts of the conversion of two men from that hospital. Bob and his wife sat with Giant and Alec's wife, not even trying to hide their joy and thanksgiving to our great God.

Chapter 15

ZIMBABWE
WAR STORIES

How the TIC TOC Club Was Formed

I feasted on the book, then the film, titled *Chariots of Fire*." Eric Liddell's story confirmed once again that our Lord can use sport or whatever else we give over to Him. Through squash, I was meeting business and professional men and women. Squash fitted my busy lifestyle. I could do a full day's work and, at five o'clock three or four times a week, meet at the courts and complete the game and the shower within the hour. Evening meetings were hardly ever interrupted. I met Chris Sewell in a league game, and he asked whether we could play once a week. We became close friends. He was puzzled about the term *missionary* and grilled me on that as a calling. I was delighted that he was the detective chief inspector and grilled him on past interesting cases. I love whodunnits. He felt religiously that he was doing enough to get into God's good books but kept asking what I meant by a relationship of faith with God. As the cross and the resurrection came into focus, I could see faith dawning. I was not the only one having input into his life, and he began to see clearly that Jesus Christ was all He claimed to be.

Soon after this, I heard that Chris was sick in bed, so I went over to visit him. From his Sherlock Holmes–like pipe, the room filled with smoke. He had a crate of beers beside him and kept filling his glass. Sitting on their big double bed with his Bible open, with great conviction, he said, "Roy, I'm reading the book of Acts. It's bloody marvelous."

"It sure is," I said. "Did you know, Chris, that it is an unfinished book, and we ordinary believers today have the privilege of following Jesus as they did and writing more stories of what He can do in this world." As I walked out to my car, I said, "Lord, thank You for his enthusiasm and that it is not my job to point to any of his negative habits."

His repentance led to a sharp reaction from his wife, Helga. I felt privileged to be invited for a luncheon but soon discovered it was not about food. With eyes flashing, she went on the attack. For Helga, religion was an intensely personal thing, and she was alarmed at the influence faith was having on her husband. The discussions covered many topics and tears. In time, the Lord brought Helga to the point of understanding and repentance. They became one of the most fruitful and effective couples in our country.

Chris started what he called the TIC TOC Club in the police headquarters in Umtali (Mutare). Before very long, there were six of his black detectives who had made a commitment to Christ. They met on most days before work for a brief Bible study and prayer. They were a truly delightful and enthusiastic group. Together, they decided that their methods of interrogation must change. From the violence of hitting the criminals' heads against the wall, they devised a thoughtful methodology that surprisingly gave them more information than they had ever had before. TIC stands for "take in criminals," and TOC for "turn out Christians." It did not always work, but there was fruit.

Chris challenged me about deepening my prison ministry, which helped me immensely when it came to reaching the man who murdered my sister and enriched us as a couple to prove God in that challenging environment. In our local prison in Umtali (Mutare), I was surprised to hear that the headmaster of our Biriiri Secondary

School, Marcus Chibisa, had been incarcerated. Having participated in the Chibisa's wedding, we were very close. One night, the freedom fighters had come to their home at the school. They put a gun to his head and said that if he made any move to contact authorities, his life and the life of his wife and children would be at risk. In the next couple of days, they carefully selected about seventy grade twelve boys and girls and took them across the border into Mozambique for training. When Marcus reported to the authorities, they said he must have been in sympathy with the freedom fighters. I made contact with the authorities and told them that they had made a gigantic mistake and asked them what they would have done if there had been a gun at their heads and a threat against their whole family. They were keeping a firm eye on me too because I fraternized so deeply with the black population. But God! How amazing is our Heavenly Father.

I met with Marcus most days, and we studied the prison epistles. He walks deeply with God and had the conviction that he was there for a purpose. There were many young prisoners, so he taught every day. He preached every Sunday and had a couple of Bible studies going. I was visiting a white man in that prison by the name of Peter Grimbeck. He was alcoholic and had burnt down his own house and was convicted of arson. His wife, Brenda, wanted him to have the opportunity of hearing the good news, so after meeting with Marcus, I also met with Peter. One day, as we met, I could see that he was angry. "Roy," he said, "they have put me in a cell with a black guy."

"What is his name, Peter?" I asked.

"Marcus somebody," he said.

"Marcus is one of my closest friends, Peter. You should listen to what he says."

Three weeks later, Peter emerged beaming from his cell and said, "You know who my best friend is, Roy? It's Marcus."

"Why do you say that?" I asked.

"Last night, he led me to Christ."

Marcus and I had been praying together for Peter and rejoiced in what God had done. When Peter completed his sentence, he stayed in our home for three months, and Gwyn and I had the privilege of discipling him.

Chris also asked me to participate in a Bible study in the home of the provincial commissioner of police. It was a delight to help disciple Mike and Molly Ann Day; Gwyn and I had already had the privilege of teaching both their daughters at the Girls' High School. They became lifelong friends, and one of their daughters went to Afghanistan as a missionary nurse while the Taliban were still in power. She and her husband are still preparing folk for service in those hard-to-reach countries. Through the years, the Lord has taken Mike and Molly Ann to different locations. They quickly became the right and left arms of the leadership of their local fellowship. We visited them in each location and gave all the glory back to our God.

Having participated in Billy Graham crusades in Zambia and Canada, it was a privilege to be asked to chair the Howard Jones crusade for the whole of our province of Manicaland. My right-hand man on that committee was Chris Sewell. His administrative skills came to the fore, and we put together a multiracial, multicultural, and multidenominational grouping. Roy Gustafson brought a team and helped us with counselor training. Howard Jones was their first black evangelist. Our meetings in the Sakubva Stadium drew bigger crowds than soccer fixtures. Hundreds were counseled, and for two years after the crusade, we followed up on inquirers. The BG organization said that more people were integrated into local churches, percentage-wise, than any crusade up to that time. Thank You, Lord.

Chris was so excited, "Roy," he said, "God is calling Helga and me into full-time service. Africa Enterprise has invited us to join their team. Would you pray with us?"

What a mixture of emotions we felt. Of course, we would pray, but how would we ever get by without them in their mushrooming ministries in Umtali (Mutare)? Africa Enterprise was enriched for many years as Chris and Helga served all over Africa in stratified evangelism. They came twice to Zimbabwe for *Mutare for Jesus* and *Harare for Jesus*. Their workers flew in from all over Africa and trained local volunteers on how to reach every stratum of our societies. For three weeks, we were in teams that reached out to schools, hospitals, prisons, police, city businesses, factories, municipalities, street children, and others. They even had a presidential breakfast and reached out to the leadership of our land. Fruit abounded, and God was glorified. After that, God led them back to Zimbabwe to promote the Alpha course and lay leadership programs. Thank You, Lord, for their servant obedience.

Road to Rusitu

Pastor Watson Rufasha was one of the greatest soul winners I have ever met. As senior pastor at Sakubva, church growth was at an all-time high. Carpenters worked hard to provide seating for new converts, but there was joy as we celebrated the fruit. Traveling to appointments was dangerous. Did we travel fast to avoid ambush or slow to look out for land mines? The general rule was, fast on main roads and slow on rural roads. The executives of the church and mission were having special consultations at Rusitu. The first 120 kilometers was fast; the last 30, slow as we noticed evidence of digging on the bush road. Yes, we asked for the Lord's angels to have charge over us, but we were also seeking to be watchful. Pastor Rufasha's nose was right up against the windshield. When he saw some evidence of digging, he would shout right, right or left, left.

What we did not know was that coming up behind us was a mine-clearing vehicle called a Pookie. When we got to Rusitu, he came up behind us and asked who had been traveling in the blue VW Beetle? "You should be dead," he said. "You missed two mines by a fraction of an inch, and a third one, you hit the side of it and brought it aboveground." He added that the mines were antitank and boosted. The engine would have been retrieved six hundred meters away, and he added that body parts would not be recognizable without DNA testing. Not sure that it matters whether you are dead or very dead! We were able to witness to that soldier and then give praise and thanks to the Lord, our Protector. All that day, we listened to the sounds of combat in the Ngorima Valley. While others were pursuing their agendas in war, we were privileged to pursue

His agenda in evangelism and discipleship. There is nothing quite like war to sharpen our listening faculties and to soften the hearts of all the inhabitants of the land. There was much reaping from every segment of society during those precarious days.

Headman Mutseta

We had no work there and no plans to start anything in the district of Zimunya, but once every week, Pastor Rufasha and I got through it as quickly as we could en route to the Burma Valley where we had churches at Valhalla and Msapa. I managed the schools in the district on behalf of the local farmers. Zimunya was famous for a sect called the City of God (Guta ra Jehovah). Mai MuChaza was the African version of Jesus Christ. She claimed to have died in the area and, on the third day, was raised from the dead. They offered healing in her name. They majored on helping couples who could not fall pregnant. The wife would be set up in a special little home. Lots of ritual surrounded the home, and at night, special "angels" who would have intercourse with her would visit her. Men around the world find it hard to admit to the likelihood of them being impotent or responsible for their inability to have children, so this gives this sect the opportunity in a percentage of the cases to claim special healing powers. In the early days, they had quite a bit of traction but started losing credibility as knowledge increased.

One day, my VW had a flat tire in Zimunya. With the fear of ambush, we rushed to get the repair completed. Our heartbeat increased as a man emerged from the bush. No problem, he was friendly and even helpful. "Why," he asked, "do I see this car go by every week at such great speed?" He had heard about our work in the Burma Valley and challenged us to start a work in Zimunya. He assured us that in his particular area, it was safe, and so we gave time each week to visit him and started a little church in his home. His name was Headman Mutseta, and he and his wife responded fairly quickly to the gospel invitation. The numbers began to multiply. They proved to be a godly and available couple, quickly taking responsibility for the spiritual needs of their area. Our church spread to three other locations.

As the war closed in, it became increasingly dangerous to venture into their area, so we arranged a training session for them to understand the gospel recording playback machine. Once a month, they got a new set of batteries and four sets of messages in ChiManyika. At the beginning, Headman Mutseta would listen and listen and then go and speak the messages. If he did not have the time to prepare, he would play the tapes in the different areas. The Word of God spread. One day, a group of "freedom fighters" surrounded his home and accused him of communicating with government authorities using the playback recorder. They said he was a sellout, and they were going to kill him. He explained to them that this recorder could only play back the Christian gospel messages they received and was incapable of further communication. When he confessed to being a Christian, they said, "We are not going to kill you for being a sellout but for being a Christian." Headman Mutseta said, "For being a sellout, I refuse to die, but for being a Christian, I do not refuse."

We would never have known how he died if Mai Mutseta, his wife, had not walked the more than thirty kilometers to Sakubva from Zimunya. We knew we were on holy ground as she spoke. "He died just like Stephen." She was weeping and said, "There were no shots fired. They beat him to death with their rifle butts. As he went down, he raised his hands and said, 'Father, forgive these young men. They do not know what they are doing.' He died quietly and quickly, just like Stephen." Strangely enough, when the war was over, a group of four men, smartly dressed in suits, knocked on our door. I invited them in. They did not tell me who they represented, and I did not ask. They asked me if I knew Headman Mutseta. When I affirmed that I did, they asked me if I knew how he died. I told them I did know. They did not want to know what story I had heard, but this was what they stated: "We do not know what you have heard. We just want to tell you that he died of a sickness." I turned to my poor Shona to answer, "Mwari anoziva zva akafa!" (God knows how he died.)

Building the Church at Dangamvura

When the vision came for building a church in the sprawling township of Dangamvura, there were suggestions that we should wait for the end of the war. The first major hurdle was to be assigned a property. The Umtali (Mutare) town planner's name was John Barlow. He was a stickler for procedure and not impressed with our passion for the Lord. I had no idea about his passion for the game of cricket, but I saw him in the crowd at a cricket match and went and sat next to him. We discussed the game in depth, and respect grew. The next time I went to his office, he took out the town plans for Dangamvura and gave me first choice on a site. In answer to prayer, money came in from the people of Dangamvura, Sakubva, and from overseas. When the money ran out, we stopped building.

We never went into debt and initially met in a lean-to on the property. We started meeting in the building as soon as the roof was on. The next Sunday, we noticed that the roofing was riddled with bullet holes. The civil war was raging in that area. We were not the target and so were not concerned about another attack. The huge job of painting had begun, and all the supplies were being kept locked up in the church. The baptismal place was finished, and we filled it with four feet of water to check for any leaks. It was the middle of winter. The night guard slept in a shack adjoining the church. A noise in the church awakened him. The intruder was busy hauling out tins of paint, varnish, nails, and other building supplies. In the dark, the night guard chased him round and round the inside of the church; then he went to the rooms behind the main auditorium. A scream pierced the cold darkness; the thief had unwittingly plunged into the freezing water of the baptismal pool. The guard tied up the young man and brought him a blanket to stop him from shaking. He spoke to him of the evils of theft, and after ascertaining that all the property was restored and that this was a first offense, he invited him to church the next Sunday and released him.

The Teacher Training College was right on the way to Dangamvura. We had prayed a lot about getting in there. As the saying went, "Reach a teacher, and you reach a thousand." The vice principal was a Gerald McCulloch. He and his wife, Annette, were Christians and trained teachers from Northern Ireland. There were some keen Christians among the students, and Gerald asked if I could come in with some serious Bible training on a Saturday night. I was already training all our teachers in the Burma Valley, so this was a delightful addition. The Saturday night dance and movie gave the students choice. Serious Bible teaching for three hours was demanding, and we were content with the eleven or twelve students who signed up. Gerald helped out, and so did Phineas Dube when he was passing through. There were others too, like David Cunningham, head of Scripture Union, who helped out. Our numbers kept rising until a few years later, 124 students were signed up.

In 1978, Roy Gustafson of the Billy Graham organization brought a young man by the name of David Hill to Zimbabwe. He had been used in crusades in the States, and because of his background in the occult, they thought he might connect with folk who had a background in witchcraft. They were right. David was the son of an American army general. David was enrolled in training at his father's insistence. He went AWOL and used his razor-sharp brain in the gambling world to become very rich. His lifestyle began to deteriorate, and he became heavily involved in the drug world as a pusher and a user. This led him to the world of the occult, and he climbed quickly, becoming a high priest. He took the oath, which he wrote in his own blood, "I give myself to you, Satan, for time and for eternity." He told us that he was on a mountain outside of São Paulo in Brazil when he encountered Satan. He was laughing at him. His kingdom was the kingdom of death, and as he looked at his own broken dissipated body, he realized that death was just around the corner for him.

The only Christian in his family was his grandfather. He remembered two things he had said to him as a boy. "God so loved the world that He gave His only Son, that whoever would believe in Him would not perish but have everlasting life." The other memory was from a song: "Amazing grace, how sweet the sound, that saved a wretch like me. I once was lost, but now I'm found, was blind but now I see." On that mountain, he called out to the Lord, "Have I gone too far with the oath I made with Satan? Would You forgive me and save me from this death?" He went back to his hotel. In the drawer, he found a Gideon Bible. He began to read it. He felt hungry and, for the first time in months, went for real food in the dining room. Back in his room, he devoured scripture and, with his photographic mind, began to hide it away in his heart. He continued this process for days. His health came back. His appetite for drugs and drink were gone.

Where can I find a Christian? What is a Christian? The only name he could think of was Billy Graham. He found his address in North Carolina, caught a plane, hired a car, and drove out to Billy's residence. He knocked on the door. It was Billy himself who answered. He told Billy his story. He seemed to understand it better than he did himself. He became a guest at the Graham residence and received discipleship training from both Billy and his wife, Ruth. How did they process the wild story that he told? Actually, everybody who receives the forgiveness of Christ becomes unshackled and has a story to tell. Not too many months later, he had the privilege of sharing his story in a number of crusades. Lucifer would not be happy about such testimonies. Fortunately, the decision was made to send David out to Africa with Roy Gustafson, one of the Graham associates.

I was nervous when I saw David—tall, blonde, steel-blue eyes, a shirt that screamed against the simplicity of the multicultural crowd that had gathered in the Queens Hall in Umtali (Mutare). Please, Lord, not a showman from America! I was wrong. Roy Gustafson introduced him, and he spoke for over an hour. His exposition of the Word and testimony were true. As I listened to him, I could only think of the group at the Teachers' Training College in Mutare. He spoke again there a few days later for over an hour. With his occult background, his understanding of African witchcraft was uncanny. Passages of Scripture rang out. One man asked me afterward, "How does he know so much about our traditional religion?"

I questioned David about this the next day when we went up to the Vumba to relax before the evening service. The decisions that were recorded that night enlarged our Saturday grouping. We loved it that appetites were increased. There was a hunger for God and an expectation of meeting Him. His presence was so real. The students who received three hours of training every Saturday night for three years began to write back to me from where they were posted as teachers throughout Zimbabwe. They brought Christ into the class-room; they were often the only preachers in the local church and the superintendent of the Sunday school. Most of them also got involved in Scripture Union activities. Some went on to higher education and taught in universities or in the teachers' colleges. The yeast of God works quietly but so effectively.

Chapter 16

MORE WAR STORIES

Chipinge and Middle Sabi

While planting churches in these two areas in wartime, there were a few incidents that stand out. The basis for this outreach came from a development in the Burma Valley. Pastor Rufasha, knowing of my total commitment to work with black churches in Zimbabwe, challenged me with these words: "Our churches in Sakubva, Dangamvura, and Burma Valley are full and growing. You were born in this country. If some of your white brothers could come to faith, maybe their attitude to their labor force would improve, and they would pay them better." I vehemently defended my singular approach but, in prayer, told the Lord that I would be available if He opened the door. That very day I, as manager of schools, had to report to Herman and Anna Vorster about a change in staff. I had no idea that his elderly dying dad, riddled with cancer, was a keen Christian and had challenged his son, Herman, to invite me to conduct a Bible study for farmers in the valley. Rupert and Pru Hildebrand were already committed Christians, and through our Thursday evening Bible study, God triggered faith. Discipleship training included lessons in attitude to and payment of labor. *Respect* was a keyword. Just calling a married man Baba and his wife Mai was like magic. Salary adjustments brought long lines of others seeking employment.

Herman's uncle Franz Kruger, driving past the headmaster of Valhalla's, Daniel Chiwarawara's, house, found me seated at their table for the midday meal. In anger, he told me that if he ever found me in such a compromising situation again, he would fire me. I told him that the next Friday, I would be at the same table, so he may as well get the firing job done right away. "By the way," I said, "the next manager may not be prepared to do the job without pay!" He was obviously completely out of line. Others apologized on his behalf, and I continued with the job. Imagine my joy when, about three years ago, I heard from a farmer that Franz Kruger had repented and found forgiveness at the cross of Christ. Like Franz, I found that only Jesus Christ could deliver one from negative racial thinking.

Phil and Lyn Alexandre were farming in the Chipinge district. They had come to faith in Christ and were a part of the community church that I was seeking to establish. I was supposed to be with them that Friday night but had delayed my arrival because of an important engagement in Mutare. At 9:00 p.m. that night, we were phoned from Chipinge, 160 kilometers away. Friends informed us that Phil, Lynn, and their family were under attack from freedom fighters. We immediately dropped everything to intercede for the safety of this fine young family who had given themselves totally to win and nurture Christians, black and white, in this frontline town. Half an hour later, we were able to get through to Chipinge, and Lynn's shaky voice assured us that they were all unharmed, although the house was extensively damaged. I got there the next morning and got the story firsthand from Phil's dad, then Phil, with members of the family chipping in with their insights.

An army major arrived. I saw it all again through his eyes. The fighters had chosen a rainy night, so the dogs were around the back, keeping warm from the fire of the Rhodesian boiler. It was estimated that there were nineteen or twenty men who had set up in the rockeries about twenty meters from the house. The farmstead was built completely of wood. The family, three adults and four children, one a visitor, were all in the living room; and Lynn was alone, sewing on the floor of their bedroom. The fighters opened up with automatic weapons and rifle grenades. Hundreds of armor-piercing bullets riddled the house. Rifle grenades are complex. It is attached to the front of the rifle with a special muzzle-based fitting. Once attached, the pin needs to be pulled, and a blank cartridge in the barrel is used to launch it when the trigger is pressed.

The first grenade went too high and took out a section of the roof. The second missed the window and exploded against the front of the house. The third was a perfect shot, right through the bedroom window; it tangled in the curtain just above Lynn's head. It failed to explode because the soldier had forgotten to pull the pin. The fourth grenade was attached to the rifle. The pin was pulled, but the grenade fell off the end of the rifle. The story was clearly told by all the mud in the garden. The soldier dove forward and managed, with his hands, to throw it about ten meters. It exploded, seriously wounding the soldier who had tried to launch it. Some of the other fighters also took some shrapnel. The majority must have thought that Phil was fighting back. The fumble caused them to leave behind rockets, mortars, and quite a bit of other equipment. They quickly disappeared through the hole they had made in the fence.

Three bullets were in a direct line with Sarah, their sleeping baby. Anyone of those three would have killed Sarah. I can still hear the exclamation of the major as it dawned on him what had actually happened. There were many bullets that went through not just that second wall into Sarah's bedroom but right out the back. The only bullets that did not get through were those in line with her body. Phil and I helped that major to see the miracle of it all. Actually, he understood it; we just underlined it. In our service the next morning, a very thankful, excited dad and husband gave thanks to God for the miracle of deliverance. This is the passage Phil read: "I think you ought to know, dear brothers, about the hard time we went through in Asia (Africa). We were really crushed and overwhelmed and feared we would never live through it. We felt we were doomed to die and saw how powerless we were to help ourselves, but that was good, for then we put everything into the hands of God, who alone could save us, for he can even raise the dead. And He did help us and saved us from a terrible death, yes, and we expect him to do it again and again.

But you must help us too by praying for us" (2 Corinthians 1:8–11, Living Bible).

Phil also ran a butchery in Chipinge. After a morning service, he asked, "What did you mean when you said God not only wants your personal lives, but he wants us to hand over our businesses to him? I have two businesses, a farm and a butchery. How do I do that?" I explained, and then we went down to the butchery and, by prayer, handed over each section to the Lord. We did the same for the farm. About three weeks later, I got a call from Phil. "Roy," he said, "remember I handed over my butchery to the Lord? Well, last night, we had gale-force winds, and he has taken the roof off."

I knew he had insurance to cover the roof repairs, but as he said, that would take ages for a settlement. Without a roof, the cold room could not operate, and the business would go under. It was also the middle of the rainy season, and Chipinge averaged a hundred inches a year. "Phil," I said, "you have the materials, and you can build. We will ask the whole Christian community to pray that it won't rain till you are finished. Put your claim in and go for it." Amazingly, it did not rain, which the rest of the farming community needed. So when they heard that there was concerted prayer, many came to help Phil finish the job. As soon as the roof was on, the rains came back. When Phil was paid out by the insurance, he was able to pay for the help he had received. He found that by honoring God in his businesses, he was able to sponsor Christian ministries around the country. He proved God as his Protector and his Provider and became a generous servant of the Lord.

The wheat farmers in Middle Sabi, hearing about the blessings in Chipinge, invited me to come to them in the afternoon for a service once a month. When that became dangerous by road, Peter Gunn picked me up in a light aircraft. That too was not without its dangers, especially in the mountainous region between Chipinge and Middle Sabi. One Sunday, a large cartridge ripped through the plane, cutting the flannel of his long trousers. We were only inches apart. He asked whether I had been hit. Having been told that when you are hit, you feel warm and soft and your hearing is shattered, I was feeling around for blood when he noticed the rip in his trousers. If you are even grazed by a bullet with that velocity, you lose consciousness. Peter had come very close to death. "Roy," he said, "could you have landed this plane if I was hit?" I would have tried but could have failed. I became a good student and, in the next few months, became adept at landing.

Where did all those folks come from? The Gunn residence was packed, and in mercy, God visited us. Peter committed his life to the Lord, but only five weeks later, he was ambushed and died in a hail of bullets at the corner of one of his wheat fields. That was a tough funeral for Peggy and for the three children: Alan, Stewart, and Sue. It was tough for me too. Peter was an outstanding husband, father, farmer, friend, and Christian. The *why* question lingered for a long time, and I am not going to even try to give answers here. Everybody from Middle Sabi was there, and they all heard his testimony. Perhaps he spoke more clearly in his death than he had in his life. It is rare on the day of a funeral to see fruit, but months and even years later, many have told me that it all started for them right there. How great are the purposes of our God.

Family Mercies

I have mentioned that we were called immature, thoughtless parents for bringing our four children to live on the front line of a war. Actually, we did not. The war came to us a couple of years after we got there, and in prayer, together as a family, the Lord taught us how to handle the dangers that were mushrooming around us. We have always felt that the safest place was the center of His will and, in daily prayer, committed our whole family to the Lord.

It was a Wednesday at 5:00 p.m. If we had known what was planned for the city of Mutare that night, we would certainly have fled to a safer place. The warning shots to tell people who had been informed came at exactly the time that people were getting off work. Everybody recognized the sound: Russian rockets seven feet long that sounded like an organ and devastating in the destruction they bring. We had taught all our children that as soon as they heard that sound, they were to find a ditch or low-lying area and lie down on their tummies. I rushed through the house. Everyone was present, except for our youngest son, Bruce. Before I could lift the phone, the explosions started.

Bruce was down by the river beside our house. His friend Philip McCulloch had asked him to look after a dog while he went home to his parents to negotiate whether he would be allowed to keep it. As soon as he heard the organ sound, Bruce, then six years old, found a low-lying place and pulled the dog in with him. The explosion was no more than twelve meters from him. Fortunately, it was where the ground sloped down to the river, so it was above him. The crater was huge. The shrapnel from it shattered the windows all along our street. When he walked into our house, he described the noise and the wind and then dissolved into uncontrollable weeping.

Another rocket landed on the main road near the police station. Hundreds of people were coming out of their workplaces. The death toll would have been very high if it had exploded! Forty-five minutes later, the jets came over and took out the silos of rockets that were to deliver the deathblow to the city of Mutare. News reports had already been prepared to tell of the annihilation. We were sent one of them. I think they had taken pictures from Beirut. By the grace of God, Mutare was still intact.

Jesus Christ loves children. Looking at our present war-torn world, how do we apply those words, "If you cause one of these little one to stumble, it would be better for him or her that a millstone be tied," or "Let the little children come to me in their ones and twos and thousands and millions; do not stop them, the kingdom of heaven belongs to them"? That is good news from the Creator and shames us in our pride and greed as we build our little kingdoms on this earth and, either physically or sexually, abuse little children or kill the unborn.

Repeated attacks on the city resulted in minimal casualties and collateral damage. After every attack, the black and white Christians of the city gathered in the park for a thanksgiving service. One weekend, we went as a family to Harare, leaving Douglas behind because he had a rugby match on the Saturday. Our frightened son phoned us on that Saturday night as Mutare came under attack. Our normal routine was to meet as a family to pray, along with the dog in our passage, which I had purposefully sandbagged to give him a little extra protection. That night, Doug would be alone there with the dog. As our family gathered for prayer on behalf of Doug, Janice was the first to pray, "Lord," she prayed, "if Doug is going to be all right, would you please help me to stop shaking?" I was watching and praying and noticed that Janice, in the next moments, became completely calm. Our prayer turned to praise as we witnessed such a direct answer. We did not have the slightest doubt that Doug was going to be safe.

Chapter 17

AFTER THE WAR
WAS OVER

Chimanimani

The war was over. Robert Mugabe was elected the first Leader of Zimbabwe. All the fighters in the war were ordered to hand in their weapons. The country was going to have one united army, air force, and police. It was rumored that only outdated guns were being handed in. I was traveling in the beautiful Chimanimani mountain area on my way back to Mutare when I saw a young freedom fighter with an AK 47, hitching a ride. I imagined that he was heading for the city to hand in his weapon. I admit I was nervous when I stopped, but we had a 160-kilometer trip ahead of us, and I thought there might be an opportunity to witness.

He looked around my VW Beetle and saw my Bible on the backseat. He asked two questions in perfect English: "Are you a Christian?" and "Are you a missionary?" I said yes to both. He turned on me in anger and said, "You are to blame for all the problems in this country. You have lied to our people. I have been for training overseas, and I now know that there is no God." Then he cursed me repeatedly.

I spoke to him in my poor Shona. "You said, 'Hakuna Mwari'" (There is no God.).

"No, no, no," he said. "Mwari ariko" (God, He is there).

I understood immediately, "You have rejected the God of the white man!"

"Yes," he said.

"You have rejected the God who is a capitalist."

"Yes," he said.

"Mwari, ndi Mwari wangu" (Your God is my God).

"Ah," he said, "then we can speak. Baba Comrie, during this war, I have killed many of my own people and raped many women, and now when I try to sleep, I see terrible images. Is there anyone who can help me sleep?"

For the next two hours, I took him to that place called Calvary where the Son of Mwari took in His own body all the violence, all the blame and shame, all the rebellion. I told him that because of that rebellion, death was reigning, so to conquer death for us, the Son of Mwari entered it and overcame it. We deserved that death, but He took our place, He became our substitute. I illustrated this with many stories. Andrew (not his name) had many questions but seemed to understand.

When we got to Meikles on the main street in Mutare, he asked me to stop. I inquired as to whether we could meet again. He told me he had a lot coming up but agreed to meet at the same spot outside Meikles one week later.

I was there first when he came joyfully to meet me. "Baba Comrie, Baba Comrie, I am sleeping now." The experience of forgiveness brought a liberation that was physical, mental, emotional, and spiritual. We became firm friends.

North Koreans

I was one of the top squash players in Manicaland. In a league game, I met an army major, originally from Australia, who was now involved in training the new Zimbabwe army. One week, he was very out of sorts, and I beat him quite easily. He was angry but unwilling to say why. I was chatting with the editor of our *Mutare Post*, and she and her journalists did a bit of digging and came up with a remarkable story. I warned her of the consequences of publication, but she felt that the people of Zimbabwe needed to know. In the wee small hours of one morning, she and her journalists met the train coming from Harare. There were many army trucks lined up to whisk away the soldiers from North Korea who were arriving. They got the pictures, and in all our years in Mutare, we never saw bigger headlines, "NORTH KOREAN SOLDIERS ARRIVE." It stirred up a hornet's nest. On that same day, Jean Maitland Stewart was flown to Harare and was dismissed from the job she was doing as editor of the *Mutare Post*.

I am not here to make any allegations, but for us as missionaries, the North Koreans were an unreached people group; and for some reason, they had been brought to Zimbabwe. The politics of it all was not our concern, but we earnestly inquired of the Lord, whether He had a plan to reach out to them. Yes, He did! I was one of three delegates chosen to represent Zimbabwe at the Association of Evangelicals for Africa and Madagascar meetings in Lilongwe, the capital of Malawi. The two main speakers had both been born in North Korea; they had escaped to South Korea. There, they found forgiveness and purpose. One was pastoring a church of seventeen thousand members, and the other man said he just had a small church of three thousand. I remember putting my arm around him and saying, "Never mind."

I told them the story of the North Korean soldiers arriving in Zimbabwe. Their joy knew no bounds. We actually did a little dance together in the front of that huge auditorium, with them leading. "God has done this," they said. "It is almost impossible for us to reach them from South Korea."

"What can we do?" I said. "We do not know the language or culture, nor do we have any literature or Bibles." I did not mention how completely inaccessible they would be and how protected they would be from outside interference.

"We fly home to South Korea after this conference. We will airfreight all the Bibles and literature you will need in their language." I explained that I was not supposed to know that they were even there. It all seemed so implausible and impossible. Only God could put it together. Can you see the unmistakable hand of God in what He had already done in connecting me with these Korean pastors? I added one more plea: "Please do not send everything in one shipment and send small packages so that I can easily clear them through customs."

They flew back to Korea, and I flew back to Zimbabwe. Would they remember? Of course, they would. They were so intent on reaching those North Koreans for Jesus Christ. I did not have long to wait. A phone call came through from the customs office in Harare. "Are you expecting a consignment from Korea?" I replied in the affirmative and asked that the consignment be sent on to the customs office in our city of Mutare. That would have been normal procedure.

"Oh no," said the officer, "we would like you to come right away to Harare to explain your order." There was an obvious threat in his voice. It was already midafternoon, and Harare was a three-hour drive. Could I come the next day? The man gave me his name and the time to report. Prayer chains were still in operation from wartime, and these were all alerted. I knew that I was in deep trouble, and as I sped toward Harare, I begged the Lord for peace of heart and wisdom in communication.

As I walked prayerfully into the customs office, I thought everyone would hear the pounding of my heart. I asked by name for the customs officer. "He is gone," was the reply. "Where has he gone?" I asked. The man repeated the first statement, "Who can I see in his place?" After a delay, a name was given to me. I conversed with him in my best Shona. As he looked for the documents, I realized that he did not understand the background. I continued chatting as he went through the documentation. "Mr. Comrie, these documents appear to be in order." He stamped each page. "If you can take your truck around to the back, I will see you get help in loading." I just got to the door when he called out, "Stop, come back here!" My heart went all the way down to my boots. "I am sorry, Mr. Comrie, but you owe $46 customs duty." I took out my wallet, laid the exact amount on the desk, and waited while he wrote out a receipt. "Now you can go."

The crate had my name in capitals, REV ROY COMRIE, and written from one corner to the next was "Bibles in Korean." I tried to look as though I did this kind of transaction every week, so many thanks to those who had prayed, so much praise to our awesome God! I have no idea what happened to the man who phoned me the previous day. For weeks, I wondered whether he would come back to me, but he never did.

In the crate, there were Bibles and booklets on how to become a Christian and how to grow in the Christian life, all, of course, in Korean. I rehearsed the things God did in getting me to this point. To get these Bibles and booklets into the hands of North Korean soldiers seemed to be beyond possibility. Black chaplains were still a part of the new Zimbabwe army. Would they have access to the camp housing the North Koreans? I got in touch with folk who were able to tell me. I then met with some of those chaplains. I did not want to compromise the security of their ministries, so I needed volunteers. We all had time to pray, and the volunteers emerged. These Bibles and booklets could not just be handed out. The North Korean soldier had to be alone. It was agreed that the Bible should be opened up so that they could see their language. They used one word: *free* and *for you*. Even the officers took the Bible and two booklets. They were hidden before the chaplain left. There was not one refusal. It took a long time to complete these handouts and great patience and prayer on the part of the chaplains.

These soldiers were in Zimbabwe for almost three years when a Roman Catholic priest in the Matabeleland area reported to the United Nations that a possible genocide was going on. After the investigations, our president was told that these soldiers would have to be repatriated. We believe that every Bible and booklet was packed deeply into their kit bags and that all that literature found its way back into North Korea. It all went very quiet for about seven years. I was in a church in Ontario, sitting up front and ready to preach, when I opened the bulletin. There was an insert called "Church Around the World." The heading was, "Revival Breaks Out in North Korea." Briefly, it said that the revival started in the army barracks in the capital city and that it had spread all over the country. My heart leapt; I knew that it was true. To me, it was like a giant mathematical problem that had been conclusively solved, and at the end, someone wrote, "QED."

Chapter 18

ONTARIO BIBLE COLLEGE

The missions professor at OBC, Dr. Ebenezer Sikakane, was a Zulu from South Africa. I marveled at the kindness of the Lord in putting us together. I was teaching in the New Testament and missions departments and relished the opportunities in such a multicultural college. Only God could put a Zulu plucked out of the complications of apartheid South Africa and a white Rhodesian who had served as a missionary in war-torn Zimbabwe together. Our love and respect for each other was obvious. For those looking for authentic Christianity, there was no debate that neither of us was acting. We were simply living out the relational realities that God had taught us in Christ.

Nineteen German young people arrived that semester. They were a fine, fun-loving, but serious group who wanted to know how they could find and fulfill the purposes of God for them. We were at about the same stage of seeking to understand Canadian culture and so bonded together. Every one of them was enrolled in Perspectives on the World Christian Movement and the book of Acts, both my courses, and so we saw a lot of one another. Content in any course is so important, but it is easier to fill students' heads with accurate facts and see them get satisfactory grades rather than living out missions and seeing them get practical experience and produce spiritual fruit.

To illustrate this, I gave them the challenge of diarizing a cross-cultural contact and two semesters to submit the diary. They were puzzled, so I explained. On the first page of the diary, with its correct date, I wrote, "Today I pray that You, the living God, would lead me to a contact who belongs to a culture other than my own. Help me to be observant and obedient." I told them, "If that was your sincere prayer, that could be the only thing that was written each day for as many days as there was no answer." It was soon proved that this prayer-centered, God-honoring approach began to produce results. Reports flowed in. I met a person on the bus, and we got talking, either on the train, in a coffee shop, in a bookstore, at a friend's house, in the hospital, or during my prison ministry. We agreed to meet again. We now meet together every Friday. I found out that she was a Muslim or that he was a Hindu. We cultivated a relationship. Discussion came back to class. How can I learn more about Buddhism, atheism, Mormonism, and on and on?

One of the most gratifying things I have ever experienced as a teacher was to take in those diaries at the end of the second semester and trace the hand of God as He led students along different pathways into deep cross-cultural relationships. Many had the privilege of leading their contact into a personal relationship with Jesus Christ. Some did that in the next school year. Sometimes a contact would lead to another contact. Some said that the shallowness of their own Christianity had been revealed and led to them asking God for a deeper, more authentic walk with Him. One said that he would never ever again be without a cross-cultural contact. Strangely enough, I have never had the opportunity of doing that again in the classroom setting but have challenged many on an individual basis and know that it has worked again and again.

We are still in touch with a number of those German students. A number of love stories and weddings resulted, and the fields of the world were enriched by the obedience of many. One day, I went early to chapel and was approached by a senior student who brought a first year dressed like some of the bikers I had encountered. Sure enough, this was a biker who had come to Christ and now to OBC to learn how he could be effective as a witness. The senior student was intent on cleaning up on the appearance of the biker. I asked the biker about the vision he had, and he said it was to be effective among the biker gangs of Canada. I asked him to speak the language of the bikers and asked the senior to interpret to me what he had said. He was as in the dark as me. I asked the biker what would happen if this senior student walked in on a biker meeting. He said that he could be in some physical danger. One more question for the biker, "Could you be sure that the gang would not reject you because of your new-found faith in Jesus Christ?"

"I am meeting with them every weekend. I can't guarantee that they won't reject me," he said. "But I am building relationships and know that I have the ear of some of them already."

One more observation for the senior: "John, would you be willing to go there this weekend?"

"No way," he exclaimed.

"Neither would I. I think we should pray for Bart and leave him dressed as he is while he reaches out to his biker friends."

Thank You, Lord Jesus, for leaving Your heavenly home and identifying with this traitor race of ours, and thank You for Bart, who has learned from You about identification with biker gangs in Canada.

I never taught Ben Hegeman but met him in the context of OBC. He was working toward a master's degree at Ontario Theological Seminary. He and his wife, Christine, were hungry to be discipled in global missions. My fear was that because I was spending so much time with them and loving every minute of it, and because all our examples and challenges came from the world of Africa Evangelical Fellowship, I wanted them to be particularly clear on the subject of the lordship of Christ in missions. To do what the Lord said and not feel obligated to follow into our sphere of ministry. The letter they sent said, "We feel terrible that after all the hours you poured into our lives, we have now gone and joined SIM." Our total delight came in that they followed the lordship of Christ. Missions are not in competition with one another but are colleagues in the big picture of bringing glory to Christ. The first letter we got in 1999, when SIM and AEF merged, was from Ben and Christine to express their joy that we were now part of the same organization. Spiritually, actually, we had never been separated. What a joy to catch up with them when recently we took the Benin/Togo Spiritual Life Conference.

Their work of training trusty men and women at Bembèrèkè for six months of the year, impacting the West African leadership scene and the other half year training and preparing students in America for global outreach, is challenging.

Steve and Marcella Parr are a delightful couple. My first contact with them was also at Ontario Theological Seminary, where Steve did his first master's degree. Marcella and Gwyn had similar interests in the nursing field. As they were going to Chizera Bible Institute, where we had taught, they had all the questions, and we sought to give them as realistic a picture as possible. They were not going to stay long at Chizera, only to get a grasp on the language and culture of the Ba Kaonde, and then go and teach at the Theological College of Central Africa. They loved the teaching part but were so talented administratively that they ended up, after many years of teaching, in the top job in Zambia as field director.

We met the Parrs again when Steve was working on his second master's degree at Regent College in Vancouver. They were all set to go back to the field when they were involved in a terrible accident in North Vancouver. They were taken to different hospitals. Marcella had a broken back and was in a Stryker frame bed when I visited her. She was facing the floor, so with instruction from the nurse on duty, I lay on the floor. Never will I forget those big inquiring eyes. In total shock, she said, "Roy, what is God doing?"

"Marcella," I said with more hope than conviction, "God loves you and Steve completely and is entrusting you both with a problem far too big for any human being to understand."

From that unique position on the floor, I then drove to another hospital where an equally distraught Steve, with multiple internal injuries and the removal of his spleen, was lying in shock. It is in those moments when man's fragility stands out in stark contrast to God's sovereignty that we grapple with the weakness of our humanity and reach out in faith for His mercy and intervention. The word *impossible* keeps pushing in and from a position of utter weakness. We throw ourselves on the mercies of the Shepherd who laid down His life for His sheep. It is true, when He sends out His sheep, He always goes before them. Some of the preparation is not what we plan but ends up giving us a perspective we could not have found any other way. Steve and Marcella have proved in their entire ministry that all things do indeed work together for good to those who love God.

Back to School

In 1985, at the encouragement of our mission, I embarked on furthering my studies at Columbia International University in South Carolina. Their strong emphasis on missions attracted many to pursue their calling and preparation for missions.

Our mission allowed us to attend CIU on full missionary support. After twenty-six years on the field in Africa and assignments in Canada, and with a passion to get back, young couples seeking the mind of the Lord and the counsel of veteran missionaries surrounded us. The president of CIU, Dr. Robertson McQuilkin, had a deep passion for the heart of God and the fulfillment of the Great Commission. So many were impacted by his service and devotion to the ministry. The stature of this man was seen most dramatically when his wife, Muriel, reached the stage of Alzheimer's disease in which she needed full-time care. He resigned his position as president in order to care for his wife. Having faced many difficult and challenging decisions throughout his life, this one, he said, was easy. She had served and cared for him all their marriage, and now it was his turn to be there for her. His powerful resignation speech and book have impacted tens of thousands of people around the world.

Our studies at CIU also brought us together again with missionary colleagues Dr. Terry and Jean Hulbert and Dr. Norm and Ginnie Hoyt, who were on the faculty.

Gwyn, who had already earned her PHT (putting hubby through) sat in on the advanced counseling course taught by Dr. Bill Crabbe (brother of Larry Crabbe). I knew that if she sat the examination, she would get a better mark than me! She audited a couple of other courses, typed all my research papers, and was well on her way through the typing of my thesis when a serious problem developed with her carotid artery. The first test, which came back negative, cost $300. The next was priced at $1000. We decided to drive the thirteen hours back to Toronto where we were covered by OHIP, Ontario's health plan. We had a basement suite in the home of Cam and Elfrida Henderson. After two cups of strong coffee and a teary farewell, I drove the thirteen hours back to South Carolina.

Up till this point, all the typing of assignments had been done on a typewriter (word processor). Computers were still on the horizon, maybe not everybody's but definitely on ours. At that time, one of the best typists was still recovering from a serious illness; but when I approached her, she decided it was time to earn a little more money. She really was the best. When my thesis was ready for the final corrections, I headed back to our trailer park home to give it a final check. Suddenly a sharp warning came over the radio. A tornado was imminent, and they were warning anyone who lived in a trailer to find shelter in a sturdy building. I could hear the thunder and see the lightning. The wind began to howl. I admit I was frightened and hungry, so I headed for the nearby Burger King. As I parked, there was a clap of thunder as loud as any I had heard in Africa, and at the same time, a bolt of lightning spewed out fire as it hit the black top just outside my car. Terrified, I waited for the next clap of thunder and lightning strike. They were two seconds apart. Relieved, I grabbed my briefcase and ran for the building.

There were seven people ahead of me in the queue. The cash machine had been hit by the lightning, so the young lady attendant asked us to wait till it could be fixed. With a mountain of work awaiting me on my thesis, I suggested that we work together, writing down each order so that it could be entered when the machine was fixed. We finally got our food, and I sat down to do some serious eating and correcting. I have never eaten a hamburger and fries as cleanly as I did that day, not wanting to smudge my papers! Thankfully, the tornado left our trailer park untouched, and the city of Columbia just got the edge of that storm.

Over five hundred students graduated from the master's programs, and 71 percent of them went into full-time cross-cultural missions. Many deep relationships were built during our time at CIU.

Standing right next to me in the graduation service was a dear friend, Bart Chlan. He kept on expressing jealousy in us going back to darkest Africa. I said he needed more courage than us in going full-time into inner-city ministry among addicts and prostitutes in the USA. Our hearts were broken when, a few years later, we heard that Bart had been murdered in the pursuit of his ministry. Only heaven will reveal the courage he exhibited and the sacrifice he so willingly made in reaching those vulnerable people. Like so many times before, we were again reminded, "How precious in the sight of the Lord is the death of His saints." Among the massacred missionaries to the many other individuals who were killed in car accidents or through sickness whom we were privileged to know in Africa was now added the life of this dedicated servant from America.

Chapter 19

PASTOR AT LARGE

For fifteen years, David and Margaret Evans were doing pastoral care and teaching in AEF's eleven countries in Southern and Central Africa and the three islands off the east coast of Africa. They shared from the richness of their prayer, teaching, and administrative ministries in Rhodesia (Zimbabwe) and South Africa. Their ministry of encouragement was a blessing to us all in the Africa Evangelical Fellowship.

With retirement looming, they were much in prayer to know who should be approached to take over from them. I was finishing a master's degree at Columbia International University when the letter came. Would we pray about the possibility of taking over from them? They were big shoes to fill, and we felt our inadequacy. We had field experience, most of it in Zambia and Zimbabwe; and by prayer, we knew that this was the next door that God was opening to us.

We left Canada in May, and for the first six weeks, we traveled extensively with David, visiting and ministering in most of our Indian churches in South Africa (Evangelical Churches of South Africa). We always stayed with the people and ate curry for breakfast, lunch, and supper. Their kindness and hospitality was amazing. Fortunately, we both love curry but got curried out, and I was compelled to run many kilometers daily to cope with their kindness! Many of those friends have since gone on to be with the Lord.

My greatest friendship was with Pastor Andrew Arumugan. He was a priest in a Hindu temple in Durban. One of the members from our Umzinto church, who had also belonged to that temple and knew the bondage the monkey god imposed on every member, walked into the temple and, taking Andrew by the hand, steered him out the temple. He sat him down on a bench and lovingly led him to the cross and to the One who died there.

Andrews's conversion was as clear as that of Saul of Tarsus. When I met him that year, he had been the pastor of the Umzinto church for some years and had built it up to over a thousand members. Their vision for the Zulu population all around them led to a strong work among them. They loved Andrew, not only because of his fluency in their language but because of the authority and humility in which he lived out all the gifts and fruit of the Spirit. His Indian congregation would have laid down their lives for their beloved pastor. Such was the impact of his life on mine that I begged him for the privilege of spending quality time with him. It was then I learned that he had leukemia and was already living on borrowed time. I have met many godly men and women during our fifty-four years of ministry, but Andrew Arumugan stands out among them all. When he died, Indians, Zulus, and white folk gathered to pay their respects, and on many minds was the question, "Why, in the economy of God, was this humble, fruitful servant not allowed to live on and produce more fruit for God's glory?" Maybe if we had known God like Andrew did, we would never have doubted and asked that question. His congregations were not just listeners but well-taught laborers, and the work in Umzinto and the surrounding area continued to thrive after his death.

In that same year of 1988, our mission gave us a very difficult assignment. Could we continue our journey and go up to Zambia, where, in this fateful year, five of our folk had died in very unusual circumstances? In one head-on collision, Klaus was killed instantly. His wife, Janet, broke her back and had a much harder road to travel in caring for their children. The headmaster of our Mukinge Girls' Secondary School died in the same accident. Maybeth Henderson lost her husband, Glen; he died of an enlarged heart. Keith and Cindy Frew lost their fifteen-year-old son, Ian, to a crocodile in the Kabompo River. Ken Askey lost his wife, Ada, to cerebral malaria.

These were all close personal friends. We kept crying out to our Sovereign Shepherd, "Lord, you just take over. May the reality of your presence even in silence or that right word in season be the answer these dear folks need.

In the economy of God, that was the year where, on the way to Zambia, we met Garry Hove in Harare. I have already told that story as it related to Chris Mnguni and my sister Sheila. Now it related to grieving fellow workers as they sought to understand the other side of the embroidery as it focused on the individual dilemmas that each faced. The wrong side of the embroidery looked like random chaos and disorderly disaster. The right side of the embroidery spelled out the Sovereign Majesty and loving, caring touch of our Great Shepherd. How can the story of the tragic death of nine missionaries and their four children be answered by the miraculous salvation of nine of their murderers? How can that same story have such a profound effect on the folk we were attempting to fortress about with His comfort? It's all about the timing of God's revelation and the application of His truth to different people suffering different degrees of loss. All we knew was that God poured His oil into many hurting hearts. We give Him all the glory!

We realize now that we have spent twenty-seven years in this conference, caring, and counseling ministry among missionaries and national leadership. It has taken us to every continent in the context of AEF and since 1999 with SIM. We have also ministered in most of the home offices. Seeing the Lord restore relationships in a home office is as important as seeing them restored on a field. In the big picture, two executives at loggerheads in a home office is as destructive to the purposes of God as two doctors from different cultures unable to agree on procedure in their field hospital.

Spiritual Life Conferences brought missionaries and nationals together. Sometimes the field would set the theme; at other times, the speaker. Expectations differed. Some from a theological or academic background wanted a structured unpacking of a text or theme; others wanted a graphic, topical dealing with current issues. The apologetic approach has worked well in the last five countries where I was asked to speak on justice issues. It was especially relevant when child sex slavery issues surfaced during the actual conference. Justice issues are biblically important, but we need constant vigilance to ensure that they do not detract us from the centrality of our biblical gospel mandate. We have seen good folk sidelined by important social issues and lose their focus on the cross of Christ.

We have at times accepted conferences outside of our mission, especially in Honduras, where over thirty mission groups got together in wonderful unity. Our contacts there were Drs. Shaw and Sharon Yount, who, not able to get back into Zimbabwe, were accepted by a medical mission in Honduras. When we were invited back, over a hundred groupings were present, and amazing unity in prayer and commitment was experienced. Wycliffe Bible Translators invited me to speak eleven times at a key conference they held at their amazing center in Nampula in Mozambique. They came from all over Southern and Central Africa, determined to complete the last remaining translations in their respective countries. By the way, they completed the last translations that will ever be required in Mozambique and have sold that property in Nampula to a vital grouping from Youth with a Mission. There are no more unreached people groupings in Mozambique. I only ever dreamed of hearing that statistic in my lifetime. Even so, come, Lord Jesus!

Our South Sudan missionaries SLC 1

The best SLCs happen when there is personal prayer preparation from every participant, followed by great expectation of meeting with the living God, who can do the impossible, and a hunger and thirst for His Word and His glory. More prayer should go into the organization and administration than any other part. Inviting the wrong group to minister to your children may destroy the conference for you before it even starts. It is still true that "people do not care what you know, until they know how much you care" (anonymous). Care ministry is not delivered from the outside. It wells up from within as we acknowledge the incomparable care that comes with His presence. People are at different stages of their care ministry. This is activated as we implement every one of the passages: You must love the Lord your God with all your heart, mind, and strength. Love your neighbor. Love your enemy. And then other passages click in: "Forgive one another, encourage one another, pray for one another, stop judging one another, love one another, and bear one another's burdens." In every field, there are some with a greater sensitivity to this. When they are identified and encouraged, a conference can turn into a movement of God, and He ends up getting all the glory. He is completely unwilling to share that commodity.

The ministry of the wonderful Counselor should take place with as little fanfare as possible. You will not counsel for long if you cannot keep a confidence. Careful listening to people and to God is basic. We have benefited from some psychological training and a lot of reading in that area. Our practice, however, comes out of pastoral theology and biblical counseling. We follow the biblical, prayerful, nouthetic (direct) approach. We are not ashamed to admit when we are out of our depth and have a careful referral plan. Sometimes, when we are out of our depth, we ask the counselees to repeat their whole problem to God in prayer and should not be amazed when we hear that they have received the complete solution to their dilemma. They have often mistakenly thanked us. Jack Taylor, a close personal friend, has his doctorate in psychology. He has served in Africa and Canada. We run nameless cases by him and are amazed at how often his solutions are biblical and nouthetic. There are so many areas of counseling, and we have sought to keep up with reading and train-ing, especially in the areas of grief, trauma, and addictions. Gwyn has a continuing counseling ministry using e-mail. Of our total ministry, this is the most taxing. Deep relationships are cultivated, and through our daily, global prayer ministry, the fruits of counsel-ing are consolidated. Our thanks to the international offices of AEF and SIM, which appointed Dorothy Haile and, much later, Helen Heron, to whom we reported in these ministries.

We were encouraged by our mission to take opportunities to speak in summer conference centers in Canada. I was invited to speak once or twice each day for a week. We were allowed to have displays, so it proved to be excellent exposure for the mission. Numbers of candidates came from this ministry. One of these centers was Flim Conference Centre in Peterborough, Ontario. One particular con-ference stands out. I was given the theme and even suggested titles. The theme was revival and missions. Some of the titles were "Lord, Come as the Fire," "Lord, Come as the Wind," and "Lord, Come as the One Who Is Life After Death." In preparation, I soon found that there was abundant biblical basis for each title and arrived with a real burden to share. Just before I spoke on "Lord, Come as the Fire," the men's dormitory burnt down. Apart from the graphics from scripture on this subject, the sight and smell came into our meeting place, with testimony from those affected by it. God met with us, and there was brokenness and commitment.

Ross Pelman and his wife, Marg, were elderly and had been attending for years. He was the kind of man who, after he had listened to a message, went around to the trailers and cottages inviting folk to attend. On the Wednesday, my first appointment was a men's breakfast. I asked Ross to give his testimony. What an amazing story of the faithfulness of God. "When I die," he said, "no old-age home for me. I want to go home straight from a Bible conference center." The next day, I was speaking on "Lord, Come as the Wind." Well, that early morning, we had a tornado! The effects of it were devastating. Trees were uprooted or snapped. Trailers were smashed. There were some injuries but no deaths. No lights for the next two days. The Bible says that the fear of the Lord is the beginning of wisdom. Frankly, I was terrified. I thought that my little cottage was going to take off. I walked nervously yet with growing faith down to the chapel and spoke on "Lord, Come as the Wind." Bend us, break us, and fill us. The Lord was so real, and His presence so near.

The last day of conference came. I greeted Ross and Marg as I walked past their cottage. The director, John, was picking them up. "See you there," I said. I was nearing the chapel when John caught up with me and stopped. "Roy, Roy," he said. I knew something was wrong. Ross was sitting in the backseat of the car next to his wife, but obviously, he was no longer there. Marg looked at me sternly, "Roy, do not cancel this meeting." She knew that I was going to be speaking on "Lord, Come as the One Who Is Life After Death." It is hard to explain how meaningful that service was. Ross was dead, but he was still speaking. Jesus, who is our resurrection and life, was nearer than breathing and closer than our hands and our feet. Till she died a few years later, Marg became our prayer partner, financial supporter, and loving friend. I am so glad I'm a part of the family of God!

Zulus and Xhosas

Apartheid in South Africa was a cancer that, from 1948, legally administered inhumanity and barbarity. It adversely affected every country in Southern and Central Africa, and its legacy has not been totally eradicated. In ten years of teaching in our Bible Institute in Zambia, every first-year class asked the same question: "Has the black man been cursed by God?" It was liberating to see that they learned the truth of God's Word: that every sinner, whatever their background, is under God's curse and that Jesus became a curse for us to free everyone who repented and put their faith in the finished work of our Redeemer. Countries that legislate equality, multiculturalism, human and civil rights have got it right on paper but battle to understand the perversity of human nature. With frequent, perplexing outbreaks of racial and tribal conflict, at least they have the right to bring a conviction or seek to educate offending parties.

My work as pastor at large included ministry to both our national churches and our missionary colleagues in the various countries. Invitations abounded from our South African churches, and appointments took me into Soweto, Wattville, and other townships during those dreadful apartheid days. Usually, our national pastors would meet me outside the township. I would park my car, and we would drive in together. In a compromising situation, the pastor would get me to duck down to hide my white skin from a threatening gang. Neither he nor I was embarrassed. After a few visits, Pastor Buhlalu figured that I knew the lay of the land and could make it in on my own. Everything would have been fine, except that the road where I needed to make a left turn was blocked off, so I went to the next road, intending to go left and then left again. Unfortunately, the road I had taken angled away, and my turns brought me into a threatening area.

I saw a young man standing beside a high wall. There was a burnt-out car in the background. When he stepped out onto the road, I saw the rock in his hand and a mob of young men emerging from behind that wall. I could read their intention in their eyes. I put my foot down flat on the accelerator. They had to dive to avoid being run over. I sped away, watching rocks fall short of my car. Through the rear-view mirror, I saw upward of fifty of them cut through the row of houses. They knew that I would have to turn left and left again. As I got to the next road, I could see that my turn would take me back to them again, so I did a U-turn. A number of them saw my move, but I was ahead of them. I have never in my life driven with such fear and fury. With distance between us, I saw an elderly man and slowed. Did he know the way to Mafiko Street? He asked who lived there. When I told him, he said that he knew Pastor Buhlalu and offered to guide me. He got in, and I marveled at the kindness of the Lord in giving me such a gentle shepherd. The old man stayed to hear me preach.

When the pastor heard the story, he was very apologetic, and I never ever drove in alone again. If I had read the Sunday papers, I would have read of that smoldering car and the ambush the previous night, resulting in the death of its two occupants. During the service, the pastor pointed to a large group of young people and said that they had been part of the problem in the township, and now in Christ had become a vital part of the solution. After the preaching, those same young people surrounded me and told me that if I had stopped, I would have been killed and my car set alight. In my heart, I already knew that!

As I got to know more of our pastors, I got the invitation to speak at the annual conference. It was at Nongoma, the Zulu capital. The president, Lloyd Magewu, was a great Christian statesman—godly, humble, and wise—ably backed up by the principal of the Union Bible Institute, Albert Xaba, one of the greatest interpreters I have ever had, and a young man, Prince Ntambo, so gifted in preaching and administration. One day, I had the last morning and the first afternoon sessions. Just before lunch, Albert Xaba was exhausted and said his top eyelids wanted to have fellowship with his bottom eyelids. The next meeting after lunch, we called the graveyard session. Albert arrived back from his rest, refreshed and ready to interpret. When eyelids meet, it helps! I was speaking on a key subject, but there were a lot of tired folk on an exceedingly hot afternoon. He let them have a brief rest then suddenly bellowed, "Vuka, vuka, vuka"

(Wake up, wake up, wake up). All over that vast auditorium, people bumped their heads as they came to order. Never saw anyone sleeping after that.

On my drive in to Nongoma, I met a roadblock. The young white policeman who questioned me knew of our conference. He said, "You guys are crazy. How can you bring all those Xhosa into a Zulu area? There is going to be a bloodbath! If I was you, I would do a U-turn and go home!" I told him that, in Christ, Zulus and Xhosas and Europeans were one. "It's not the Christians you have to worry about," he said. "It's the masses out there in the township."

I was speaking four times the next day and awoke at 1:00 a.m., troubled with one of the messages. I went into the fresh air outside, and as I pondered and prayed, I heard voices. I walked toward them. There were twenty-five people in earnest intercession for our conference. I joined them. Then the story unfolded. How do you bring over a thousand Xhosa-speaking people into a Zulu area and guarantee their safety? There had been serious concern and prolonged discussion. They read 2 Chronicles 7:14: "If My people who are called by My name will humble themselves and pray and seek My face and turn from their wicked ways, then will I hear from heaven and forgive their sin and heal their land." For two weeks prior to the meeting, there were twenty-five who met for two hours, then were replaced by another twenty-five. There was twenty-four-hour coverage before, during, and for a few days after the conference. Leadership took the threat seriously, decided on this prayer strategy, and proved "that it is not by might, nor by power, but by My Spirit, says the Lord." No wonder I had so much liberty, that blessing abounded, and that protection was experienced. For me, it was a graphic from God. I had learned about giving from poverty-stricken Mozambique Christians, and now I learned the deep lesson on prayer from my South African brothers and sisters.

The next year, I was asked to speak again in Umtata. This time, over a thousand Zulu Christians were traveling to Xhosa land. There, at the entrance to the city, were the police. I got another "You're crazy" speech, so I told him how seriously our leadership took the threat and, rather than dismissing it, answered it by intensive prayer.

That appeared as weakness to him, so I heard more of the impending bloodbath. I checked into the prayer meeting again and, from the pulpit, mentioned that the greatest contribution to the blessing was not the preaching, teaching, or organization, but the presence of our living Lord who, in answer to prayer, not only protected us but filled our hungry hearts and lives. Ray Oosthuis, one of our veteran missionaries, arrived a day late; and when I chatted to him about this subject, he said that he had learned more about prayer from his African brethren than all his Bible College training put together. "Please, please, Lord, take us deeper in our learning about warfare prayer."

Chapter 20

BACK TO MALAWI

Napolo

The country of Malawi, formally known as Nyasaland, got its independence in the early 1960s. We have had missionary activity going on their way back into the early part of the last century. We have also experienced times when all the missionaries were told to leave the country. There was a great deal of church growth during those early years. Malawi seems to slice its way into Africa. It's a long, thin country, and often those who superficially study a map of this once dark continent miss it. Its eastern border is part of the great rift valley of Africa, which you can trace all the way down the eastern part of the African continent. Lake Malawi runs for almost two-thirds of the length of the whole country. The southern portion pushes like a hypodermic needle deep into the belly of Mozambique.

During the dark days when missionaries were being denied entry into Mozambique, we made Malawi a launching pad for the gospel. We had centers in places like Chididi and Lulwe, and from there, we were able to once again make contact with many of our church people and reach many unreached people groupings inside the country of Mozambique. In 1990, Gwyn and I were asked to speak at a very strategic conference. It was not just a conference for missionaries, but it was a very deep-felt need by both the missionaries and the church to come together. The theme they gave me was revival and missions. They were not thinking of sending missionaries into Mozambique at that particular time, but they were thinking of areas of Malawi that remained unreached. We had reached into the southern part in the hot Shire River valley area, and then for years, we were stuck there. Some vision had taken our missionaries to Blantyre, a big city and also into the capital city of Lilongwe, where we had built churches and Bible colleges.

Our Bible conference was unique in that everybody was there: the missionaries, all the national pastors, leaders, and their wives. We prayed, and we planned and prepared for that conference, and God met with us in a very real way. We never dreamed of the direction that the conference would take. Heaven came down, and lives were laid on the altar for the Lord. Groups from the Lulwe, Chididi, Nsanje, Bangula, Blantyre, and Lilongwe began to meet separately. We gave them questions such as, "In the next five years, by the grace of God, Lord, this is what we would like you to do through us in our area."

I personally recorded the findings of all the groupings, and because I was going regularly to Malawi and meeting with all the missionaries and regularly speaking in the church conferences, I was able to track the progress of what had been asked of the Lord. What I noted was that six years after that conference, everything they wrote down was fulfilled, and what they had purposed and planned in extension to the East, West, and up to the North was realized.

At that particular conference, one of our church leaders was a man by the name of Mr. Kansangene. He was a headmaster, a very senior man, so senior in fact that he could have the choice of any school he wanted. During that conference, he made a commitment to the Lord, which he wrote out on the commitment card we had given out. He wrote, "Lord, I give up all my own plans and purposes, all my own desires and hopes, and accept your will for my life. I give myself, my life, and all utterly to You to be Yours forever. Go on and on filling me with Your Holy Spirit. Use me as You will. Send me where you will. Work out your whole will in my life, at any cost, now and forever."

When Mr. Kansangene signed that card, he said, "Lord, because I am a senior man, I can say this is where I want to go. But now, I am just going to leave it to you and believe that you will be Lord in my life and send me to the place that You would like me to go."

Soon after this, Mr. Kansangene was appointed to a very tiny school at the foot of Mount Mulanje called Chiringa. It is a beautiful mountain range spreading out about twenty-five kilometers. Just after he and his wife and family arrived there, Napolo happened. According to the local inhabitants, it is visited every now and again by what they call a wild beast that tares at the mountain. In March 1991, it happened again. In seven locations, millions of tons of rock came tumbling down. On one fateful night, more than five thousand people were buried alive and remain entombed under the rock until this day. The rocks rolled ominously toward Mr. Kansangene's house and stopped within meters of totally destroying his dwelling. It didn't take Mr. Kansangene long to realize the enormity of the tragedy that had overtaken them.

In the wake of that tragedy, Mr. Kansangene and a small team of Christians moved out in ministry to the people who survived. A church was started under the mango trees, and on a couple of occasions, I can remember having the privilege of preaching there. From that one temporary grouping among the mango trees, a permanent church was built. From that church they started, three others were formed; and from those three, four more. They reached out and crossed the Mozambique border and started four more churches there. All this growth and fruit because one man, one headmaster, became obedient to God. He didn't tell God what he would do but asked the Lord what He wanted him to do.

The church at Chiringa is a wonderful place to go to today, and you can visit all the churches in that area. Abusa Nyahoda, a gifted evangelist, became the answer to the pastoral and evangelistic challenge. He was a man who was wonderfully used by God, along with the headmaster of the school, to establish all the works in that area. That is just an illustration of what was taking place not only in Chiringa but what was also repeated in many parts of the country of Malawi, and we give God all the glory.

The Accident That Changed My Life

A few years after the preceding story, I got a phone call from one of our Malawi missionaries. As we were flying from Zimbabwe to Malawi the following day to speak at their Spiritual Life Conference, they wondered whether I could pick up a copper clock in the shape of the map of Africa. No problem, I knew exactly where to go. It was the big clock, so I asked them to pack it well to take on the plane next day. Just as well, it was intact even after the accident. I was one block away from Coke Corner, a landmark in the industrial sites of Harare. I was in the right lane heading for a right turn at the T-junction (we drive on the left). Slightly ahead of me in the left lane was a huge tractor trailer. When the young African man driver saw that the service station on the right was selling diesel, he turned right in front of me. I had to turn with him and skidded as I braked. The back of his truck somehow attached to the back of my car and shook me like a rag doll. The back wheels of his trailer were about to go right over my car when he looked out his window and saw me. He braked, and my life was saved. His huge rig blocked the whole road. He was very apologetic, saying that it was his fault. There had been no diesel in Zimbabwe for some time. and he wanted to get in line before they were sold out.

As there was no bleeding, I thought I was okay. All traffic was blocked. We phoned the police five times. They did not have a vehicle, so the officer had to walk. The white man who owned the rig arrived, bellowed at his driver, and went off to the police station. I learned later that he had paid them off, and I was charged for the accident. I had insurance with the Automobile Association. They told me that I should just pay the fine as they had never yet won a case in court against government even with overwhelming evidence. Such was the corruption that nothing was ever recorded on my license or in their records.

No bleeding does not mean no injury. Later scans revealed that C6 and 7 of my spinal segment were badly smashed. At the conference we flew to the next day, the devastating effects of the accident became apparent. I began to experience headaches that I had only ever heard about from other people. Our Malawi team was so kind. They prayed, and I confessed my total weakness and disorientation to the Lord. The sessions went by like a blur, but because we were all calling on the Lord, He came, and testimony after testimony told of His touch and undeserved blessing. It was the very end of 1999, and we were to fly out of Malawi on January 1, 2000. Do you remember Y2K? How would computers take to the new century? Would there be a meltdown? Air Malawi was so anxious that all flights were cancelled, and we flew on January 2. I knew something was wrong. We took off and flew just above tree level and failed to get any altitude. Sure enough, after a few minutes, we circled and landed again in Lilongwe. The computer expert arrived, adjustments were made, and we successfully flew on to Harare. I heard that we were the only ones anywhere in the world to have a problem with Y2K!

Life consisted of chiropractors, physiotherapy, massage therapy, x-rays, scans, and medications. Every day I had four or five blinding headaches. I found a medication that would give me enough relief that I could preach or teach and interact before the next headache came. At that time, we were flying to South America for Spiritual Life Conferences in Peru, Chile, Paraguay, Ecuador, and Bolivia. We thought we had come to one of those rivers that was uncrossable, but encouragement letters came in from all our caring churches and friends, and we sought to focus again on the God of the impossible. My medical doctor helped me plan coping strategies. I had my thorn in the flesh and enjoyed fellowship with Paul in his writings and proved that God's grace was sufficient for me too. I studied online and discussed with my doctor the surgery to repair the damage. Even though the operation got very poor ratings, I was desperate, so my MD began to investigate possibilities.

A weekend conference in Ontario was coming up. Many of our own missionaries attended, and the whole group were very supportive. My condition was reported, and much prayer was promised. In between sessions on the Saturday, three men, two of whom I had never met, came to me with the same story. "Roy," they said, "I have had that surgery. Do not go that way. I was worse off after it than before." The third man, Milton Arnold (we had worked together in

Zambia), came in the afternoon. As he stretched out his hand to greet me, he said, "Roy, before I had that surgery, my hand was not shaking. I am weaker now than before. Find another way."

The conference closed after lunch on the Sunday, and we traveled back to Toronto. That evening, I got a call from a surgeon. This is what he said: "I heard about your conference this weekend from friends who were there. I have done that surgery for the past twenty-five years. If there is any way you can avoid it, take that path. If you absolutely have to go that way, there is one surgeon in BC that I can recommend." He gave me that name. I went back to our MD in Abbotsford with this story. "I can see a closed door," he said. "Let's consider other options." He gave me the name of a young physiotherapist whose business was actually within walking distance of our home. He was getting some excellent results with people suffering with neck and headache pain. Armed with the CT scan and x-rays, I made the appointment. Jeremy was honest: "Roy, C6 and C7 are a mess. I can work with you for a while, but my manipulations and massage will only ease the stress. Are you good at exercise?" I told him that every day of my life, I did the Canadian military 5BX adjusted routine. Traveling as much we do, we had to be able to get all the exercise we needed in a limited space. He laid out the exercises for me. He demonstrated them and then tested me. He said it would take at least six weeks to see any result.

At the six-week mark, I told my wife that I only had two headaches that day. For the first time in years, headaches were not the dominating factor. I still do these exercises most days. Actually, it's a headache that reminds me that I have missed a day. As we travel around the world, I have met many fellow sufferers and introduced them to the program. Some have benefited. Thank You, Lord, for the joy and privilege of being able once again to get to multiple countries and minister without too much pain—that is, until arthritis in the hips struck, but that's another story!

Chapter 21

MISSION PLANES

In the amazing purposes of God and to accelerate the spread of the gospel, God gave a young man, Murray Kenyon, the vision to found Mission Aviation Fellowship (MAF). Born in New Zealand, he was a World War II veteran. When he thought about the destructive power of the aircraft he had flown, he wondered, why not use airplanes to bring hope and help to those who need it, as well as bring the Good News? In 1946, he flew to America and connected with the Christian Airman's Missionary Fellowship. The UK and USA groups came together, and in 1950, MAF was born. Sister programs were started as others caught the vision. Now small and large planes in the hundreds, along with helicopters, fly into remote areas to bring doctors, medicines, and the Good News.

As a new missionary at Chizera in 1962, I was given the task of building an airstrip with strict instruction on length and camber. I think I lost about ten years of my life when the first plane to land brought with it four heavy executives. After our meetings and a wonderful meal, we watched them take off only to see the propeller crop the grass on a huge anthill at the end of the runway! Needless to say, I had to completely level that anthill and add another two hundred meters to the airstrip!

During the civil war in Angola, I had to take a flight from Windhoek to Lubango to visit our missionaries. Blaine was one of the MAF pilots. In the course of the flight, Blaine asked me if I knew a Doug Comrie.

Blaine on left

"Yes," I said, "that's my eldest son." It turned out that Doug was his flight instructor at Trinity Western University.

As we approached Lubango, Blaine was instructed to come in high over the city and maintain a holding pattern. The reason soon became obvious. A giant Russian Ilyushin transporter jet, designed to deliver heavy machinery to remote and poorly served areas, landed first, followed by a number of MIGs landing three at a time. No sooner had they landed than they disappeared into large underground bunkers alongside the runway. It didn't take long for the transporter to disgorge its cargo of antiaircraft guns, tanks, artillery, armored vehicles, and other military supplies.

Moments later, as we approached the runway, a group of WWII Spitfires came into view. I could hardly believe it. These were the planes I had studied and hoped to fly as a boy. I had an itchy finger on my camera but knew that it would be suicidal to take any pictures. All photography was forbidden in war-ravaged Angola. We later learned that the maneuverable Spitfires were more effective in the bush warfare than the faster MIGs.

Although the civil war was raging, we were able to fly into a battle-scarred Menongue to encourage Anne Culley and a traumatized church grouping. Stories of suffering and death abounded, but also stories of the miracles and grace of God. Leaving those dear folks was hard, knowing I was leaving them in such a dangerous war zone. We mobilized churches all over the world to pray for them.

I flew back to Lubango where I completed my time of ministry in Angola. On the morning I was to leave Angola, I went to the airport early. The King Air was fully booked for the flight to Windhoek in Namibia, and we were soon all gathered around the plane. Blaine arrived after picking up our passports. When you are leaving a war-torn country, you have a deep appreciation for those who are in that front line, and you also breathe a sigh of relief that you are about to be flown to the safety of a neighboring country!

While the pilots did their final checks, seven armed soldiers were carrying a man on a stretcher across the tarmac. A well-dressed woman walked beside them. There was no doubt about their destination, and we soon learned about their intention. One of the soldiers announced that they were commandeering the plane. The man on the stretcher was a very sick high-ranking military officer. The woman was his wife, and the soldiers his guard. The pilots were going to be forced to leave all of us behind and take their group to Windhoek.

My heart fell as I was speaking at a meeting that evening and then had an early connection from Windhoek to Johannesburg the next morning. Blaine and the other pilot came over to us and said, "Pray for us. We will negotiate with this group. We need wisdom and courage." Fortunately, Blaine was fluent in Portuguese.

We moved under the shade of the wing and started to pray. We could hear angry, raised voices, and the tension rose. It seemed like an age, but it was probably only seven minutes. Blaine came to us and announced his decision. "We have agreed to take out three of the seats and make room for the stretcher, and the wife of the man will be given a seat beside her husband. As we are flying to a neutral country, no soldiers will be needed to guard the sick officer." The soldiers were not happy and walked menacingly up into the plane, but the sick man barked out an order, and the armed guard meekly retreated to the main terminal. We thanked the Lord and the four who had been volunteered to give up their seats.

The group that I spoke to that night had a deep prayer interest in Angola and listened with great insight and understanding as I shared with them my visit to Angola. Thirty-six churches had sprung up on the Namibia side of the Cunene River, with refugees who had fled the Angolan war. I had the privilege of going to most of those churches, and we could hear the sounds of war even as we met. The Lord prepared a table for us in the presence of our enemies.

Arriving at Oliver Tambo Airport in Johannesburg next day, I got the bus to Pretoria. My sister Sheila's husband, John, met me and took my luggage, which included my briefcase and wallet. I had a meeting and told John that I would be dropped off at their home that evening.

Later that afternoon, around five o'clock, when I was in downtown Pretoria on Church Street, I saw two men fixing their gaze on me. I knew that I was their target, so I began to move off the sidewalk (pavement) toward the road. What I did not realize was that there were two other muggers coming up from behind. I was suddenly in the vise grip of these two men. One of them had his arm around my neck, and a knife went through the skin in line with my heart. His mouth was right next to my right ear, and in perfect English, he said, "If you shout, you are dead." I believed him!

Thankfully, my passport and wallet were safely on their way home with John, but they did take my watch and R350 before finally throwing me against the side of a building. I ended up with a five-inch cut in my arm and blood everywhere. There must have been fifty people within twenty yards of me, but no one saw a thing. I can still spot a mugger when they are on the prowl. Like a predator, they are focused on their prey. A chemist was still open, and they kindly dressed my wound and refused payment. Thank You, Lord, for Your protection during my three weeks in Angola and for the lessons I learned from those muggers and the kindness of that chemist.

Lost in the Clouds

Flying with Don Amborski was always an adventure. He rarely hesitated to swoop down on a herd of buffalo or elephant, which would add real excitement to our trip. After flying fighter jets in the Vietnam War, he now was one of our most accomplished pilots flying those little four- and six-seaters. Our fellowship was rich and deep. I flew with many mission pilots in Zambia and other parts of Africa; none exceeded Don in competency, not even his son Don Junior, who took over from his father!

On one occasion, he had to go down to South Africa to pick up a small plane and fly it back to Zambia. The red tape was incredible, but eventually, permission was granted to cross the two international borders, and Don was able to fly safely to Lusaka, the capital of Zambia. Early the next morning, he took off and headed for Mukinge in the Kasempa district. Well into the flight, the weather turned foul, and his instruments were playing up. He was lost!

Just then, he saw a man riding on a bicycle on a narrow dirt road. He came in over the man's head and landed just ahead of him. He climbed out of the plane and walked back to the man, whose eyes were very wide open and never blinked. After greeting him, Don asked him if he knew where the road went, and could he point to Kasempa?

"Mumbwa," said the man, and then he pointed toward Kasempa. The man had still not blinked. Don thanked him, climbed back into the plane, and with those two coordinates, he flew straight to Mukinge. One can only imagine the story that man told when he got home, which he probably repeated many times to his children and grandchildren.

MAF Flights in Tanzania

Tanzania has 115 languages, and you would think it would be one of the most fragmented and divided countries in Africa. Yet it has achieved a unity in its diversity that is unparalleled in any country in

Southern or Central Africa. The key to this unity is the remarkable Kiswahili language, spoken by almost every tribal group.

Under the umbrella of the missionary organization, Christian Missions in Many Lands (CMML) of Wiedenest, Germany, our mission (AEF) gained a foothold in the Mtwara and, later, Lindi areas of Southern Tanzania. My privilege was to fly in many times from Zimbabwe to encourage and counsel in both mission groupings.

Our first missionaries there were Darrell and Kristen Swanson and their two children, Matthew and Joanna. They were the ideal family for the work, but they battled with malaria (actually, no one was exempt) and, with Kristen, the debilitating effects of Epstein-Barr. Their aim was to reach the unreached Makonde, Makua, and Yao people.

On one trip, I flew with MAF from Dar es Salaam to Nanjoka where Darrell was teaching in the Bible school. I had done the trip previously from Mtwara to Mbesa, which was much shorter, but it had taken seventeen hours with the four-wheel drive engaged most of the way. So this was all joy as we weaved between the towering cumulus clouds, avoiding storms.

Two hours later, as Nanjoka (place of the snake) came into view, I saw the tall figure of Darrell waiting on the side of the narrow strip, but something was dreadfully wrong. This normally strapping man was a shadow of his normal self. Getting closer, he also looked jaundiced; and on the drive to the school, he told me that he had suffered twenty-eight consecutive bouts of malaria, and it looked as if hepatitis had also clocked in. I did not say anything to Darrell at that time, but I knew that when they went back to the States in five months, they may decide that health issues would prevent them from returning.

We were making a brief stop at the Bible school before motoring on to Mbesa, where our colleagues had a hospital, trade school, primary school, and the largest of the Kanisa la Biblia churches. For the next five days, I was the conference speaker for CMML and AEF, and the subject was spiritual warfare. The fellowship and discussions were vibrant. As I was doing final preparation for one of the sessions, I realized that Darrell's unusual health issues may be tied up with this warfare. I knew that they were about to write a prayer letter, so I suggested that the centerpiece of their letter should be an urgent request for their health. Their prayer warriors responded, and Darrell recovered his health before furlough without getting one more bout of malaria. Kristen recovered from her Epstein-Barr on furlough, and the family came back to Tanzania with renewed vision and energy. The unmistakable hand of God was at work.

Chapter 22

* • *

MOZAMBIQUE MINISTRY

When we took on the ministry of pastor at large, we decide to make our home in Harare and, from there, travel to all fourteen countries in which our mission, the Africa Evangelical Fellowship, served. This meant we were away a lot, but we tried as best we could to give a fourteenth of our time to Zimbabwe. The people were perplexed but gracious. But with the war raging in Mozambique, our missionaries and church folk needed special care. I will highlight just a couple of the incidents during that trying time.

Crossing the border from Zimbabwe to Mozambique in war-time was never pleasant—hours of questions, checks, and double-checks. The conference center was not that far from the border, but we still had to go through numerous police checks. They all wanted money, but instead we handed out gospel tracts or gospels of John telling them God's Word was worth more than silver and gold. It was in their language, and they were delighted. Only heaven will reveal whether that seed of His Word brought new life to them.

The conference was amazing. Over three thousand came, as they had the previous year. What a privilege to be their speaker again and to see God working in answer to prayer. Some traveled three weeks to get there. In most areas, it was impossible to travel during the day because of the war, so they would sleep in a hidden place and then travel cautiously during the night. They risked their lives for opportunities like this.

There were so many stories of gladness and sadness, triumph and tragedy, that were shared often late into the night. Before we went to bed that first night, we heard the devastating news that five of the pastors who had been with us the year before had been killed by RENAMO, the anti-Communist rebel group that sought to overthrow the government. All their wives and families, now widows and orphans, were at the conference to tell the story. It felt very much like being a part of the early church.

Christians in Mozambique had a unique way of taking an offering. Here at the conference, buckets were placed at the front. When the time comes for the offering to be taken, they stand and begin to sing while making their way in an orderly fashion to the front, where they place their offering in the buckets. It doesn't take long for the buckets to be filled. There is always such joy and purpose in their giving.

At the time, Mozambique was rated as the poorest country on the planet, so I was staggered when informed of the total. But what happened next taught me how little I knew of sacrificial giving. A man got up and told the stories of the five pastors who had been killed in the previous year. They had been killed in the line of faithfully proclaiming the gospel. Then the question was asked, "What are we going to do for the widows and orphans who are here with us?"

Spontaneously, the people began to speak together; and before long, the singing started. And once again, they shuffled to the emptied buckets and once again filled them. How could such poor people give so much, I wondered? It didn't take long for me to understand. Most of the folk coming to the conference where they were not adversely affected by the war were able to catch a bus. They knew if they gave their bus fares as an offering, it would mean a much longer journey home on foot, but they reasoned that these widows needed the money more than they did. God's unmistakable hand was making sure that those who needed help were given it and assured them of His love for them. The lessons were clear: God has no spoiled children. There is cost, joy, and privilege in carrying out His commission in our Jerusalem, our Judea, our Samaria, and to the uttermost parts of the earth. It was a lesson on sacrificial giving I shall never forget.

Burn Out

It was the day after my sister Heather's funeral. Gwyn and I left for a five-week ministry trip to Mauritius, Reunion, and Madagascar. We were to discover that constant travel, wall-to-wall ministry, and the death of a close family member were a recipe for revealing our own vulnerability. The indignity of "burn out" came out of left field. Neither of us saw it coming, nor did we recognize some of the signposts along the way. We had been to these islands a number of times. It was hard but rewarding work.

Mauritius is called the Pearl or Star of the Indian Ocean. The Dutch got there in 1638 and left in 1710. The French came in 1715 and were conquered by Britain in 1810. The British handed over independence to the island in 1968, and in time, they became a republic within the Commonwealth of Nations. The official language is English, but Creole, Hindi, and even Chinese are widely spoken.

There were two British ladies who came with Child Evangelism Fellowship (CEF) in the 1950s to work among the children. The adult population showed no interest in Christianity but was delighted to have someone bring interest and education to their children. Over time, those children grew up with the Word of God, committed themselves to the Lord, married one another, and formed strong Christian homes. The British ladies, upon retirement, contacted the Africa Evangelical Fellowship to see if we could help to take over the work. We were blessed to build on the firm foundation established by CEF. Church planting began under Wilf and Marie Green (our director) in the '60s, followed in succession by Ginger and Dulcie Wright, Dave and Elwanda Fields, Richard and Carol Waddell, and Kamyl and Lorraine Cadinouche.

Kamyl Cadinouche was born on Mauritius to an Indian Muslim father and his French wife. At the age of nineteen, disillusionment set in, and he told his father that he was leaving the island and immigrating to Canada, where he would make his fortune.

Once in Canada and still angry and unsettled, a friend invited him to go to church, and it was at Calvary Church in Toronto that he heard for the first time the good news about Jesus Christ. It wasn't long before he gave his life to Christ. His great thirst and expectations led him to study for four years at Ontario Bible College, where he met Lorraine and eventually married her.

God gave them a clear vision to reach Mauritius in a church-planting capacity. Fluent in Creole, Hindi, and English, this godly, gifted family brought vitality and vision as churches were strengthened, new churches started, and the Bible school encouraged to not only produce men and women for ministry in Mauritius but, as it turned out, to graduate folk who would be used in ministries around the world.

On one of the trips, I commented that as a man with a Canadian driving license, he drove with all the skill and flare of a local man. "Roy," he reminded me, "I am a local man." After many years, Kamyl and Lorraine returned with their two children to pastor a church in Toronto and to work among international students in Canadian universities. They saw many of them mobilized in Christian service around the world.

We were scheduled for three weeks' ministry in Mauritius, then eight days in Reunion, and then all the missionaries from both islands would fly to Antananarivo, the capital of Madagascar. Our missionaries from Mandritsara, led by Dr. David and Jane Mann, met us at the conference center. Their journey by road would take a lot longer than ours by air. I am going to leave to your imagination the hectic month of ministry before we landed. I had seven messages to give at this conference, and I was well prepared.

Those times are very interactive, and discussion and prayer followed each message. Unexpectedly, I caught myself in some rather unusual behavior. I would go alone to our room, curl up, and weep uncontrollably. My own diagnosis was that I was stressed out, and there was nothing that a few days' rest would not cure. I should have shared it with Gwyn, but I was too ashamed. The unusual behavior continued. Somehow I got through six messages, with one to go. I slipped away to the room to do final preparation, but to my horror, I could not put two sentences together. My message was together on paper, but I could not put it together in my mind. I curled up and wept again. Suddenly Gwyn came into the room, saw the tears, and asked a number of questions. I told her, "I no longer want to be a missionary, and I no longer want to be married to you."

She fled from the room to find Dr. David Mann and told him everything. He came into our room and announced, "Roy, you are not responsible for tomorrow. Others will be sharing and, you do not even need to be there."

I have forgotten what else he said. He gave me some medication, and I slept through the night and through breakfast. I did not go to the final meeting. It was just as well as they spent a portion of it praying for me. Later, when David came back to the room, he explained his diagnosis and made me promise that as soon as we got back to Zimbabwe, I was to see our doctor. The encouragement from everyone at the conference and promise of prayer was humbling. Before we left Madagascar, I apologized to the Lord and to my wife for my irrational statements.

Back in Harare and after a few days of rest, I felt so much better, and so I put off that appointment with the doctor. But another conference was looming. The international conference of our AEF was meeting in Harare, and they had requested that I be the speaker. I threw myself into the preparation and was excited about the privilege of presentation and interaction with our leadership from around the world.

I never even got through the first message. Those same rotten waves that I remembered from Madagascar swept over me. I broke down into a pathetic bundle, so ashamed that I had not followed through on professional advice. I deserved rebuke, but I got sympathy. I was told later that they had the divided message times between them and spoke on the theme of being burned out. Many confessed that they had also been skating on the edge and that the theme from scripture turned out to be a timely word. I saw my doctor that same day. My friend Dr. Derek Pringle was very stern and forthright, and I became an obedient, humble patient.

I was able to trace the hand of God clearly through those dark days and ended up thanking God for the experience. Why? Because our ministry, after the merger with SIM, spread to over seventy countries. I will not mention any names, but on four continents, Gwyn and I were able to recognize burn out in some of the missionaries and counsel accordingly. If it is not caught in time, it can take great leaders out of the work permanently. In one of our fields, our missionary knew he was in burn out but thought that the field leader would not understand. They were from different cultures. We contacted the field leader by radio. He had already concluded that the person in question was in burn out but was afraid of being misunderstood. The evacuation from the field was carried out with great care and kindness. It's a battle out there, and in the warfare, many are honorably wounded.

Chapter 23

❖ • ❖

WILSON FEMAYI AND PRISON FELLOWSHIP (ZIMBABWE)

What set Chuck Colson apart as a presidential aid to Nixon was that he became his "axeman" and therefore contributed to Watergate. In prison, Colson came to the end of himself and the beginning of repentance and living faith. The ultimate result was the formation of Prison Fellowship International. The movement spread through prisons in North America and eventually to the ends of the earth.

The effects were felt in Zimbabwe in 1986 when two murderers, Moffat Karambamuchero of Mount Darwin and Peter Mandianike of Mutare, were coming to the end of serving long-term sentences in the notorious Chikurubi maximum-security prison. What set these two men apart from other prisoners was that they had repented and had their hearts turned toward God. They used every opportunity to worship and invite other inmates to join them in experiencing the redeeming power of Jesus Christ.

One night, the Lord spoke to Peter and Moffat in a similar and special way. Next morning, when they met at their usual prayer point, they decided to write down on toilet tissue (the only paper available) what God had communicated to them. They were both to serve in prison ministry. I could read the excitement in Peter's voice as he related this story. So in 1987, Prison Fellowship Zimbabwe (PFZ) was born, built upon the precepts of mercy, forgiveness, love, and spiritual deliverance. Under a governing board, it became a national Christian movement of reconciliation and restoration to all involved in crime or affected by it. The redemptive power and transforming love of Jesus Christ is being proclaimed to prisoners, ex-prisoners, victims and their families, and those assisting in the establishment of a fair and effective justice system.

Wrongly Accused

Wilson Femayi had no thought of connecting with PFZ. In fact, he did not know they even existed. In August 2009, it was my privilege to be one of the speakers at the Annual Revival Conference of our national church in Zimbabwe. Wilson Femayi walked in, after being released from one of Zimbabwe's terrifying prisons. A tall good-looking man, he was as skinny as a rake. He asked to see me in between sessions and told me his story.

God called Wilson into full-time ministry and then opened the door for him to study at our Rusitu Bible College. From the beginning, he was opposed by part of his non-Christian extended family. They could not see any money in a pastor's salary and kept voicing their objections and trying to force his hand. He persevered and graduated with a three-year diploma. Soon after his graduation, this same family set up a girl and, with bitterness, accused him of rape. The police came, handcuffed him, and threw him into an overcrowded prison. It was the middle of winter. The toilets were all blocked, the stench overwhelming, and his clothes taken away. He lay there naked in the filth and cried out to God, "You know that I am not guilty. Why have You allowed me to suffer like this?" It was then he began to think of God's Word and, God spoke in his mind and heart clearly. *This is My appointment for you. You will be My witness in this place.* He recalled the story of Joseph and was encouraged. He apologized to the Lord for his self-pity and prayed for wisdom in witness. Over the next days, weeks, and months, he cultivated relationships with his fellow prisoners and guards. He sowed the seeds of the Word, and there was an overwhelming response in repentance and faith.

Jabulani Nkani (left) and Wilson Femayi (right)

One story stands out because we had the privilege of meeting Jabulani Nkani. An accountant by profession, he decided on a quick way to get rich by copying the signature of another rich man. He was caught and sentenced to an eleven-year term of imprisonment for forgery. He ended up in the same cell as Wilson Femayi. In time, Wilson led him to Calvary and explained why and how Jesus took his place and was crucified as his substitute. Jabulani became not only a disciple of the Lord Jesus Christ but also the trusted friend of Wilson. When Wilson was freed, they wondered about ever seeing each other again. What a moment when Jabulani walked in to Prison Fellowship, looking for a bed in the halfway house. Their recognition and their joy knew no bounds as they embraced. Jabulani ended up helping them in their accounting department until he was able to find a full-time job. Gwyn and I were visiting Prison Fellowship

Zimbabwe on that very day Jabulani Nkani walked in. We bonded immediately, knowing that God had done an eternal work in his life.

As investigations into Wilson's case under a legal firm hired by his brother Pastor Never Femayi continued, the family who had accused him became afraid and fled Zimbabwe. It was discovered that it had been a setup, and the police came to the prison to apologize to Wilson and set him free. He was grateful that he had been acquitted but pleaded for permission to stay on and continue his ministry. This was denied, and he tearfully said good-bye to a host of newborn babes in Christ and committed the leadership to a few whom he had discipled.

On August 21, 2009, at Biriiri, Wilson told me that he felt God was calling him into full-time prison ministry. What should he do? I told him that the same God who had so purposefully loved and led him during his incarceration would show him what to do and where to go. Wilson volunteered at the prison in Mutare and was fulfilled until the lawyers sent in their bill for services rendered for $5,000. Wilson got a legal work permit for South Africa and began to pay back the lawyers. It looked like an impossible task!

We shared his story with many in conferences and churches. There was a lot of interest but no practical help, until on our way back from conferences in Alberta, when we stopped overnight with a godly couple who were supporting us. A couple of days after leaving them, Steve phoned to say that he could not get Wilson Femayi out of his mind. Would it help if they paid the whole amount? "No," I said, "it may complicate things, until I get a written statement to say that no more money would be sought after the $5,000 was paid." We were able to get in touch with the legal firm who gave written assurance that the money would pay for the fees in the High Court of Zimbabwe to completely clear the name of Wilson and that no more funds would be sought. Thank You, Lord, for generous servants and the lovely gift of giving. Wilson Femayi is now married to Judith, and they have a ten-month-old son, Daniel.

For the last five years, Wilson has been working full-time for Prison Fellowship Zimbabwe. Their prayerful initiatives have brought salvation to many.

The children at Chikurubi Prison

Children of prisoners are being educated and evangelized, and lives are being touched even in the maximum-security section at Chikurubi. If only we could double up on everything and reach all forty-six prisons within this needy land. We have the access. We just need the vision and provision, and thousands more will know that they have come under the blessings our Lord loves to pour out when His children agree to be clean, overflowing channels, obeying the challenge of 2 Chronicles 7:14: "If my people, who are called by my name, will humble themselves and pray and seek my face and turn from their wicked ways, then will I hear from heaven, forgive their sin, and heal their land."

Chapter 24

TODAY FOR TOMORROW (NHASI ZVE MANGWANA)

Chris Maphosa and team

The AIDS pandemic rampaged through Africa and the world. At the end of 2015, there were 36.7 million people living worldwide with HIV-AIDS; 1.8 million were children under fifteen. By June 2016, 18.2 million were accessing antiretrovirals. The fact is that there is still no cure, though the picture painted in the two-thirds world is vastly different to the first world, where it is said to be under control. Hundreds of Christian and other organizations became involved with orphans and vulnerable children. We have alarming figures for children at risk as soldiers, in sex slavery, and child labor. Fortunately, a growing number of people are alerted and active in seeking lasting solutions. I will draw back the curtain on just one project that has become a real movement of God; it is called Today for Tomorrow. The God who is in charge of international affairs is raising up many such movements, and to Him, all praise and worship goes.

Looking back, I see visionaries and practitioners who, through research and trial, established foundations upon which others have built. A pediatrician, Dr. Geoff Foster (Gwyn and I worked closely with him in our years of working in Mutare), synchronized the medical facts with biblical truth and galvanized people not only in Zimbabwe but also throughout Southern and Central Africa into following this biblical and medical approach. He published most of the first usable materials. Tim and Trish Barrow and Graham and Jessie Haddad, missionaries with AEF, followed the vision God gave them. Chris and Nancy Maphosa, after eleven years in the pastorate and the completion of Chris's master's degree, brought vision, fulfillment, and the passage of this project into an amazing movement of God. I have a UNAIDS and UNICEF report from 2006. Our mission SIM is working in twenty-six of the countries in Africa mentioned by them. The total number of orphans in our countries is 36,629,000. With the biblical emphasis on orphans and widows, we are all benefitting from the research that brings understanding of paternal and maternal conditions and double orphans and the clarity we need in seeing their immense importance to God.

Camps coming out of Today for Tomorrow ministry

It is still difficult for us to realize that Chris and Nancy only have one other full-time worker, Lina Murozve, and that, together, they have trained six hundred plus volunteers. These folks go through rigorous training and are prayed over and handpicked. On a weekly basis, they reach over fifty thousand children. They have a four-year curriculum and teacher's manuals written by Chris. Children are evangelized and discipled, trained in trustworthiness, respect, and caring. What a privilege for Gwyn and for me to have visited them all in Zimbabwe on a yearly basis for the last twelve years and to see those small beginnings accelerate into the movement it has become today.

In one government school we visited recently, the vice principal said that since the introduction of T4T, the students' grades in other subjects had improved, along with the general behavior. In that school, eleven of the teachers on staff were also teaching as volunteers in T4T. Our churches in Zimbabwe were excited, and new churches were being planted as a direct result of children taking their faith back home and being salt and light to their parents. From tiny beginnings, it grew in Zimbabwe and has now spread to five locations in South Africa, as well as Swaziland, Botswana, Angola, and Namibia. Four countries are knocking on the door. The program has been going long enough for us to see children making good choices, marrying one another, and forming Christian homes. Many graduates go on to become volunteers.

With a handicapped child of their own, Chris and Nancy have a keen eye on meeting the needs of every individual or grouping with disabilities. Nobody has ever been able to point out a child in need. They have a special gift from God in those identifications and will not rest until the child knows of their love and the love of the Father for them, and then the provision of a wheelchair or whatever would be practical in their circumstances.

Chapter 25

PART 2 OF THE STORY OF SHEILA AND CHRIS MNGUNI FROM 2012

Pastor Nġwenya—Servant, Soldier, Ambassador of Jesus Christ

It was just over a year before we were back in South Africa. In March 2012, I was again able to visit with Chris Mnguni. This time, the Lord turned the embroidery over, and I had a glimpse of His continuing handiwork in Chris's life. We had been praying for a couple of years now for someone to be able to go into murder plus on a regular basis. God superabundantly answered that prayer.

Figure 1 Roy and Pastor Ngwenya at prison entrance

On March 5, 2012, I met Pastor Ngwenya. He had been appointed to murder plus, where Chris Mnguni was imprisoned. Every Monday, he would visit the prison, and it just so happened that Monday was the day that I chose to visit Chris, and so we met. Our fellowship was rich and deep as we shared our journeys with God, and I learned how he came to be at the prison. It happened after a terrifying incident in which he was hijacked in his car in Westville. The hijackers dragged him from his car onto the road and shot him several times. Two of the bullets went through his groin and shattered his right hipbone. Mercifully, he lost consciousness and woke up in a hospital bed. The hospital authorities did not know whom to call because his wallet containing identification had been stolen, along with his car, cell phone, and other items. It was while he was recovering in hospital that God spoke to him, renewing his call to part-time prison ministry.

After an hour together, he announced that it was time for us to go into the meeting and that I was to be the preacher that day. What a privilege. You would not have been able to measure my joy when I was greeted by Chris, the three other murderers whom I knew, and more than seventy others. All were rejoicing in their relationship with the Lord. I spoke for thirty-five minutes and tried to sit down, thinking that I should leave time for Pastor Ngwenya, but they insisted that there was plenty of time as they were all there for life, and Pastor Ngwenya was there every Monday. They were hungry for the Word, and their response was so real and their questions so vital.

What a joy after this meeting to meet with Chris Mnguni for another hour. I had the help of David Mkhize, a man who had already served a big chunk of his life sentence. In January of this year, he had committed his life to Christ and has been almost like a father to Chris. His story is that even though he had been at the scene of the crime of a murder and he was found guilty as an accomplice, he was not actually the murderer. His desire was to help Pastor Ngwenya in his ministry wherever he can once he was released from prison.

The Miracle of Forgiveness

Another conference brought Gwyn and I to South Africa for the second time in 2012, so I made hurried plans to meet Pastor Ngwenya on July 2. Even though I got right in to murder plus, my paperwork was incomplete, and I was turned back. I was no more than thirty meters from the meeting place, where almost a hundred people were waiting for me to come and speak. It was so frustrating. But I learned a valuable lesson about not having all the paperwork in order. Pastor Ngwenya took the meeting and reported more fruit. Thank You, Lord, that it was only me with my nose out of joint!

Another trip to South Africa was planned for 2013, and I made arrangements to visit the prison on February 13; this time, with my paperwork in order! I arrived early, at 8:30 a.m., for the meeting. Over eighty men—all convicted for murder—were waiting for us. Chaplain Andy Munro accompanied Pastor Ngwenya and me.

After a time of singing, Chris asked if he could speak. With great difficulty and many tears, he told of the night that he murdered Sheila and of how much he regretted that night, when, as an escaped convict, he was high on drugs and did what he did. I wept as I heard again the horrors of that night. Chris told us of the miracle of forgiveness and how I had reached out to him, giving him a Bible and telling him of the love of God and His willingness to forgive. When he had finished, I walked over and gave him a hug.

I was able to share from the Word for over an hour. The prisoner who interpreted for me was a university graduate. He had become mature in his faith and outstanding in his leadership among the growing group of believers. Pastor Ngwenya has concentrated on training keymen like him to take leadership in the "cell" groups.

After I had finished speaking, many of the men responded to my invitation to get right with God. Together with Pastor Ngwenya and Andy Munro, we spent three hours counseling the men. One young man told us that two men had framed him and that he was unjustly accused of the murder. In the same meeting were those two men who had framed him, and they came up to him and asked that he forgive them for implicating him in the murder. The warden was also in the meeting and heard that confession. He said that he had just witnessed authentic Christianity in a very real way and was astounded. There is hope that he will get that young man a new trial. We give the Lord all the glory for the outcome of that morning. Pastor Ngwenya and I have since developed a very close relationship that grows each time we meet.

A Door Opens to Women Prisoners

During 2013, my wife and I were in nine countries in ministry. We had planned for five countries, but it grew, and we felt privileged and fulfilled. What we did not know was that in one of those countries, I had picked up amoebic dysentery. It hid for a while but began to manifest in April 2014. I suffered appalling dysentery for over six months, and in the middle of that, on September 22, I had a total hip replacement. Unfortunately, complications developed, and doubt clouded upcoming travel plans.

However, both our doctor and our surgeon were behind a ministry trip planned to South Africa and Zimbabwe for two months from

February to April 2015. At this time of writing, we have just returned with much pain but with a story to tell how, in our weakness, the Lord has strengthened our relationship with Chris Mnguni and how He opened a door to speak in the women's prison at Westville.

On March 9 2015, Pastor Ngwenya returned to South Africa after nearly three weeks of ministry in Edmonton, Alberta, Canada, and was in time to accompany me to meet with Chris Mnguni and the large group of prisoners who were now regulars. Many of the prison staff were becoming more attentive and taking notice of the positive changes in the men. The wild-eyed young man who murdered Sheila was now five years old as a disciple of Christ, with a steady eye and a gentle and quiet spirit. Once again, I marveled at the hunger and thirst these men have for the living truth of God. Their insights are profound, and they continue to be fruitful witnesses within the prison community. As I hugged Chris in greeting, I gave thanks to God for the amazing fruit that came out of that dark, dark day back in 2007.

After the meeting, we counseled many men. One stands out in particular. I recognized him from past visits and knew of his commitment but was ignorant of his background. His first name is Pasan, a Zulu. He got a degree in economics from a university in South Africa then went on for a master's in economics in the USA. His "gospel," he told me, was the gospel of entitlement. He had no time for anything "Christian." He had it all: a beautiful wife, Pumi, and two children, Mfundo (learned one) and Bayanda (special). Their home, their car, their lifestyle were designed for total avoidance of anything to do with God. Then came the fateful weekend party, the alcohol, the drugs, the scene, the murder, and waking up in prison. His world fell apart. But it was there in prison that Pasan heard of forgiveness and saw it demonstrated. It was there he came to a living faith. He was enabled to ask his wife, Pumi, and two children for forgiveness. With their support, he is hoping for parole by 2021.

Chris has been continuing his schooling with the oversight of an inmate who is also a teacher, and he hopes to get him through grade twelve in the next four years. We praise God, who is able to do immeasurably more than we could ask or think. As you read this book, pray for these men who have found new hope and life in Christ and for prison chaplains everywhere, that God would use them to his glory.

I did not think I could ever have a day that would surpass the ones I had experienced in murder plus with the men, but March 10 in the women's prison was just such a day. Pastor Ngwenya asked me to speak and relate the story of Sheila and Chris to the women. We were coming up on Easter, and as I was reading in 1 Corinthians 15 and Luke 24 and the other gospels, the message I had to give came in to focus.

The Zulu woman warden ushered us in and repeatedly shouted out the invitation to attend, giving the inmates the choice to attend or not.

I started my address to them with a rather graphic story from 1964, when as a I, young man, and my lovely wife and two small sons were expecting our third child within the month. Then came the mamba bite. History was against me. No one in our country of Zambia had ever survived a mamba bite, and the paralysis was progressing rapidly through my body. This was a time for very specific prayer over the general type of prayer (see Chapter 5). When I did finally survive those first critical days of uncertainty, I was told that I would never walk again. I was devastated. But I was soon to discover firsthand that prayer really does change things, and in time, even the paralysis reversed. And on January 2, 1965, I held our newborn darling daughter, Janice, in my arms. I felt like I had come back from the dead. The experience emphasized our human frailty in the face of the tough circumstances that confront us in life. Such is His mercy.

I looked into the eyes of the mainly young group of convicted women, all facing a life sentence for murder. Most of them had murdered their husbands and some an uncle who had repeatedly raped them. Local culture is important but difficult to understand, and the Western suggestion that before the woman resorts to murder, she should just leave the relationship is much easier said than done.

The hopelessness, sadness, and helplessness that I saw in their eyes immediately reminded me of the story I had read that morning in Luke 24. It was the third day after Good Friday, and the women went very early to the tomb. Their experiences brought great fear before faith dawned, but when they excitedly told the disciples that Jesus had risen from the dead and shared the infallible proofs they had witnessed, they were shocked at their reaction. Verse 11 says, "But they [the disciples] did not believe the women, because their words seemed to them like nonsense."

Two of the men who had expressed that sentiment then set out on the Emmaus road on their eleven-kilometer journey home. As the Risen Christ came alongside them, their eyes were tight shut. Their blindness, sadness, and hopelessness were on open display. They were downcast. Jesus was walking and talking with them, but they did not recognize him until He broke the bread with them in their home. Was it because they saw the nail prints in His hands? No sooner did they realize who He was, but we're told He disappeared from their sight. With their eyes wide open, they asked each other, "Were not our hearts burning within us while He talked with us on the road and opened the scriptures to us?"

Though it was dark and dangerous, they returned the eleven kilometers to Jerusalem and were in time to witness yet another appearance of the Risen Christ. Not only were their eyes open, now He opened their minds so they could understand what they had never understood before: "The Christ will suffer and rise from the dead on the third day and repentance and forgiveness of sins will be preached in His Name to all nations." Here we were in one of those "nations," sharing the same story about the Risen Christ.

I told these convicted women that there was no way Pastor Ngwenya or I could help them in their desperate circumstances but that we had not come alone. The same Jesus who had come alongside those hopeless, foolish disciples and delivered them from their help-lessness and caused their hearts to burn was with us and fully under-stood and loved every woman seated before Him. As I illustrated these resurrection truths with the story of Sheila, Chris Mnguni, and the scores of men in murder plus, Pastor Ngwenya and I witnessed a gradual change. The hopelessness turned to hope. The hardness turned to repentance. Hope and repentance gave way to tears, and we were humbled in the presence of the Risen Christ as He accomplished His purposes in the hearts of these needy ladies.

As we sat down, the first to leap to her feet was the lady warden. It took a lot of courage, but this is what she said: "The reason you came today was for me. In order for me to be forgiven, I need to forgive the man who killed my brother. I have resisted this for years, but now I know that God will give me courage to do this. Please pray for me as I long for His forgiveness."

It was humbling and overwhelming to see what happened next. So much brokenness and so many crying out. There was no way that we could adequately counsel everyone, but we know that the Risen Christ who touched those ladies and began such a good work in them is able to bring it to completion (Philippians 1:6).

Later, Pastor Ngwenya wrote, "The prisoners in both the male and female sections are still talking about those wonderful days. They were blessed in an extraordinary way. Please pray for me as I do the follow-up."

The Lord Adds to the Number

After finishing a seminar at Mission Fest in Vancouver on the "Power of Forgiveness" in January 2016, I suddenly began to doubt all that had happened at the women's prison. We were leaving a few days later to fly back to Africa for ministry and a visit to the prisons. What if it had just been an emotional response? Sure, there had been fruit, but would it remain?

On the day of our scheduled visit, we were up early and battled the traffic to get to the prison gates on time. I was rebuking fear and doubt but felt its grip. The lady warden greeted us with joy. When we had left her on our previous visit, she had said that she was going immediately to see the man who murdered her brother. As she told us of that visit, I was overjoyed and felt the doubts and fear begin to recede.

All the women from the previous year met us, now full of joy, with many others I had not yet met. Their singing was worshipful and joyful. God gave me great liberty in speaking His Word. How I love that verse in Acts, "And the Lord added to their number those who were being saved." As Paul said to the Corinthian believers, "Such is the confidence that we have through Christ toward God. Not that we are sufficient in ourselves to claim anything as coming from us, but our sufficiency is from God, who has made us competent to be ministers of a new covenant, not of the letter but of the Spirit. For the letter kills, but the Spirit gives life."

Hardly out of her teens, Nicolette was incarcerated in 2014 along with her brother for the murder of their parents. A family feud led them to seek the advice of a guru involved in the occult. We are not sure of the details of the murder, but as Gwyn and I spoke to Nicolette, we realized that she had already begun to listen and obey the Word of God. Rejection from every family member and all of society was inevitable; such is the horror of this crime. As we counseled Nicolette and loved her in Jesus's name, she clung to Gwyn and was encouraged. Currently, she is writing songs and poems to God, with deep thanks for His mercy and grace toward her. She has a burden for her brother, who has not yet come out to any of our meetings on the men's side.

By the way that guru who misled these two teens got a double life sentence. We are praying for an opportunity to meet with him.

We had gone into the men's prison the previous day. Pastor Ngwenya, full of faith and expectation, led the way. The music was great. Chris Mnguni, now nearly seven years old in Christ, could not hide his joy as we embraced. The welcome from scores of individuals and from the corporate body of redeemed murderers was moving. Their hunger for the Lord and His Word and their expectation of meeting the Risen Christ and of receiving undeserved blessings makes the foolishness of preaching an incomparable privilege.

One of the men I counseled, CD, followed by a long Zulu name, blessed me with his understanding of freedom. "Before I met the Lord," he told us, "freedom to me was living in a free society and being free, therefore, to capture, rape, and murder. After I was caught and incarcerated, deprived of all my freedoms, I came to hear you and Pastor Ngwenya speak. I repented and began to understand what true freedom is all about. If the Son of God, Jesus Christ, sets you free, you will be free indeed. I no longer envied the lives of those who boasted of their freedom and are bound by violence, lust, and pride. I am incarcerated but free in His Spirit to help my fellow prisoners to experience the freedom Jesus Christ gives. And when parole comes for me, maybe in 2021, I am being discipled now to be able to help others understand its true meaning." Wow!

As I look back on this amazing journey the Lord took us on following Sheila's death, I am humbled and amazed at how God works in the smallest of details to the obstacles that seem so overwhelming and impossible to overcome. When we agree to see and participate in what God is doing, we can only stand back in amazement. The unmistakable hand of God can be seen in every step of this journey.

In October and November 2016, we were back. A church and an individual had sent in enough money to cover our trip, and a Canadian pastor and his wife wanted a firsthand experience of Zimbabwe in preparation for bringing a team to work with Today for Tomorrow and maybe others. My doctor, surgeon, and specialist gave me clearance, so did SIM.

Our ministry time in South Africa was special, but with an added hitch: my left hip gave in, and after two sleepless nights, I had added a pile of pain medication. Two days before we arrived at the men's prison, Chris Mnguni was involved in an altercation. He was carrying a big tray with tea and boiling water to one of the wardens. Another prisoner walked by and shoved him. The tray, tea, and boiling water went flying, and the other prisoner got burnt. He blamed Chris. The standard procedure kicked in, and both were dispatched to separate prisons. Chris will make an appeal from there. He phones Pastor Ngwenya most days, missing the body of Christ at Westville but praying for new opportunities where he is.

I bonded very closely with the rest of the men. We had conversions and interesting counseling sessions. One stood out. I wrote of Pasan, with his bachelor's and master's in business administration. He was married to Pumi with two sons, Fundo and Bayanda. All I knew was that in following his gospel of entitlement and excessive party lifestyle, under the influence of alcohol and drugs, he got into an argument with one of his best friends and ended up killing him. He woke up in prison. His next words to me were, "I thank God for bringing me to prison, for it was here in 2012 that I heard the message of forgiveness and found that blessing for myself."

I asked Pasan how Pumi and their two sons, Mfundo and Bayanda, were doing. He asked how I knew their names, and when I told him that we had been praying for them regularly since he first mentioned them in 2012 after his conversion, he was amazed. New life in Christ meant loving and caring for one another. He then brought me up to date on Pumi and their two sons. Mfundo has recently graduated as a lawyer, and Bayanda is in the early stages of his legal degree. With God's help and great sacrifice, Pumi has labored to see their boys get the best possible training. With parole just around the corner, Pasan can hardly wait to get out into the workplace again and become the husband, father, and Christian leader he believes God wants him to be.

I began this book and now am closing it off with the story of Chris and Sheila. I told Chris that I believed that when the time came for him to enter heaven, one of the first to meet him would be Sheila (his head went right down between his knees in pain and anguish). She would tell him that she was there because of the grace, mercy, and forgiveness of God and His provision for her in Christ. She would tell him that she was glad her brother had learned about forgiveness and been enabled to forgive him and that he had been able to find peace and forgiveness with God. She would tell him that she personally forgave him the moment she met the Lord. The last thing that I said to Chris, I took from Paul's loving advice to the Galatians: "The only thing that counts is faith, expressing itself through love." As the beautiful bride of Christ being prepared for her Bridegroom, we need to become deeply aware of the unmistakable hand of God moving in the midst of our utter unworthiness and ultimately bringing all the glory to Him. Please, Lord, increase our faith and make it the kind that expresses itself through love.

The rest of the story of Chris Mnguni and all those other murderers who have turned to Christ—and of Pastor Ngwenya, Gwyn and I—is still to be written. And if I know my God, the best is still to come!

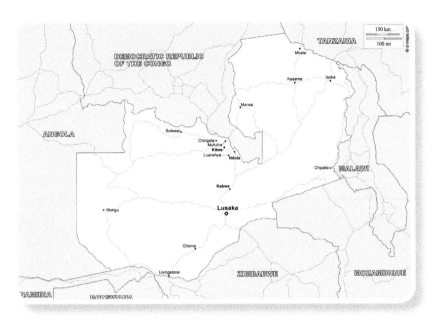

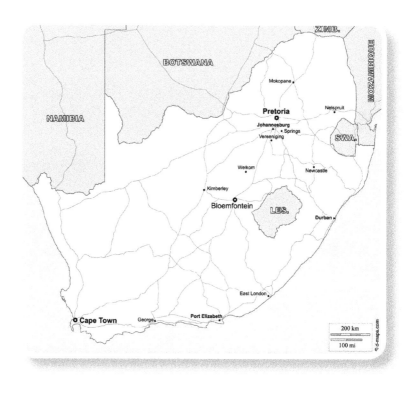